Boys, Early Literacy and Children's Rights in a Postcolonial Context

This book explores boys' underachievement in literacy in early years education in Malta, using the dual lens of children's rights and postcolonial theory.

The author confronts issues in literacy attainment, early literacy learning and transitions to formal schooling with a case study from Malta. The book includes the voices of young boys who experience formal education from the age of five and adds a fresh perspective to existing literature in this area. Drawing on empirical research, the book traces the impact of foundational ideas of gender and early childhood, and makes practical recommendations to help young children experience socially just literacy education.

This timely text will be highly relevant for researchers, educators and policymakers in the fields of literacy education, early childhood education, postcolonial education and children's rights.

Charmaine Bonello is a lecturer in early childhood and primary education at the University of Malta. As a postcolonial female academic, together with her past professional experiences in education, she contributes unique insights and insider gender, literacy and early childhood education perspectives to the decolonisation debate and children's rights advocacy.

Routledge Research in Literacy Education

This series provides cutting-edge research relating to the teaching and learning of literacy. Volumes provide coverage of a broad range of topics, theories, and issues from around the world, and contribute to developments in the field.

Recent titles in the series include:

Reconceptualizing the Writing Practices of Multilingual Youth
Towards a Symbiotic Approach to In- and Out-of-School Writing
Youngjoo Yi

International Perspectives on Writing Curricula and Development
A Cross-Case Comparison
Edited by Jill V Jeffery and Judy M Parr

Code-Switching as a Pedagogical Tool in Bilingual Classrooms
Insights from a Secondary STEM Classroom in Zimbabwe
Miriam Chitiga

Argument Writing as a Supplemental Literacy Intervention for At-Risk Youth
Using Design Based Research to Develop a Knowledge Building Literacy Course
Margaret Sheehy and Donna M. Scanlon

Boys, Early Literacy and Children's Rights in a Postcolonial Context
A Case Study from Malta
Charmaine Bonello

For a complete list of titles in this series, please visit www.routledge.com/Routledge-Research-in-Literacy-Education/book-series/RRLIT.

Boys, Early Literacy and Children's Rights in a Postcolonial Context

A Case Study from Malta

Charmaine Bonello

LONDON AND NEW YORK

First published 2022
by Routledge
4 Park Square, Milton Park, Abingdon, Oxon OX14 4RN

and by Routledge
605 Third Avenue, New York, NY 10158

Routledge is an imprint of the Taylor & Francis Group, an informa business

© 2022 Charmaine Bonello

The right of Charmaine Bonello to be identified as author of this work has been asserted in accordance with sections 77 and 78 of the Copyright, Designs and Patents Act 1988.

British Library Cataloguing-in-Publication Data
A catalogue record for this book is available from the British Library

Library of Congress Cataloging-in-Publication Data
A catalog record has been requested for this book

ISBN: 9780367646202 (hbk)
ISBN: 9780367646271 (pbk)
ISBN: 9781003125525 (ebk)

DOI: 10.4324/9781003125525

Typeset in Times New Roman
by Apex CoVantage, LLC

I dedicate this work to the young boys who participated in the study presented in this book. You empowered me to keep going and acting in the best interest of all children.

Contents

Figures

Tables

About the Author

Charmaine Bonello is a lecturer in early childhood and primary education at the University of Malta. She teaches courses in early childhood education and care and primary education. She has worked as an education officer (Early Years and Quality Assurance) within the Ministry for Education and Employment (MEDE), a senior manager at the National Literacy Agency and as a kindergarten educator, primary school and literacy teacher in the Maltese education system. Charmaine has also worked as a policymaker at the European level in areas concerning quality in early childhood education and care (ECEC). She is also the co-founder and Vice President of the Early Childhood Development Association of Malta (ECDAM) and one of the Members of the Board of Administrators of The Malta Foundation for the Wellbeing of Society.

Foreword

The expression 'boys will be boys', the online Cambridge Dictionary tells us, is 'said to emphasize that people should not be surprised when boys or men act in a rough or noisy way because this is part of the male character'. The rock band Miami Sound Machine had already, back in 1985, produced a song that affirmed 'Boys will be boys / bad boy, bad boy'. Need we say more?

It feels as if compulsory schooling, and its prequel, starting from the very early years of childcare and kindergarten, is moving further away from providing an educational milieu conducive to the education of boys. Is it because of the obsession and compulsion to make the youngest of children school-ready, socialised to sit for long hours and drilled to read and write from pre-primary level? Is it because the teaching profession has become heavily feminised, and most so at the very early levels of schooling and pre-schooling? Is it because the contemporary fad with educational assessment is now rationalising and measuring what had been there and known all along: that boys score weaker than girls in certain areas?

For the (probably adult) readers of this book, we need only remind you of the (perhaps many) times when, in your childhood, you earnestly wished that you were adults. The authoritarian stance of some parents, guardians, older relatives and schoolteachers would elicit feelings of embarrassment, hopelessness and failure, which in turn could have led to a loss of self-confidence, assertiveness and engagement. We therefore need not be surprised when children react to such power games and displays by becoming despondent, losing interest in school and instead perfecting those behavioural traits that make them stand out and respected amongst their peers. Especially for boys, they may even fetishise being illiterate, uncouth, mischievous and naughty. In this perverse vicious cycle, such traits match the stereotype, condemning the child at school to being identified with that cadre of students who are deemed losers. Later on in life, these same students, now adolescents, are likely to shirk school at the first opportunity, and seek early employment and other escapes from such oppressive milieux which seem programmed to bring out the worst, rather than the best, in them. And, in the post-COVID-19 age that we are now navigating, we can only wonder how those many months and spells of lockdown and remote teaching have exacerbated the alienation of certain children from schooling, its regimen and its developmental prospects.

We are excited to recommend this book to you, but not so much for (yet again) illustrating the symbolic violence that certain children, and boys especially, suffer and bear at the hands of the institution of education, starting from the very early years. This much is known and well documented. The dangers of making educational practices match the requirements and desires of the service providers, rather than those of the service users, is palpable; it is a challenge for all service agencies. Educators, like Charmaine Bonello, must continue to 'fight against the machine' and institutional inertia, championing the rights of those that are most weak and vulnerable. The formation of new cadres of teachers, professional development programmes and building communities of practices to provide support and mentorship at school level and promote justice in such settings, are critical considerations here.

The freshness and originality that we feel Charmaine brings to the narrative is twofold. The first is micro. The personal touch. The boys in her focus are subjects and agentic. In spite of their young age, they are already cognisant of the parameters of their situation and feel the boredom and discomfort, even the physical pain, of trying to fit into the system's expectations and accompanying material resources. One of many vivid memories of the stories of this book deals with the sore hands and fingers of a young boy, obliged to come to terms with his pencil.

The second is macro. The dynamics of classroom and kindergarten practice in the small island state of Malta are strategically contextualised within a theory of postcolonialism. Here, then, is not just a singular case study, but another former British colony that continues to champion early literacy and celebrate what is an academically driven curriculum, decades after its own political independence. We know that such curricula can reward highflyers and achievers; they also provide educational passports for those who would wish to work abroad. But they also simultaneously produce failures who end up blaming themselves for their disappointing performances at school and associated examinations. Such a conceptual framework exposes the quasi-hegemonic power of existing pedagogic practices and explains their stubborn endurance into the 21st-century.

In order to validly contemplate new possibilities of collective action, those concerned or engaged with educational systems in countries and settings like Malta need to acknowledge colonial legacies and their consequences in policy, discourse and practice. And they would do well to listen to the boys in their care, and what makes them happy and excited.

Finally, we are privileged to count Charmaine not just as our colleague at the University of Malta, but also as our friend. She has the energy and zeal that come from being a relatively latecomer to higher education, and she has already left her mark with the various organisations she has spent time with. With this, her first book, she provides a powerful statement in favour of children's rights and advocacy. Here is a text that serves as an excellent resource for a challenging and timely conversation about the practices of early childhood education, which – as the boys herein would argue – should not be driven by concerns about handwriting, forming letters of the alphabet correctly, or drawing within the margin.

Anna and Godfrey Baldacchino
October 2021

Preface

Soon after completing my doctoral studies at the University of Sheffield in 2019, I got the idea to write this book. The young boys' views on early literacy learning in Maltese schools kept echoing in my head. I wondered whether other boys, or girls, might be experiencing the same in diverse contexts and cultures around the world. I felt an inner urge to take further action and share these voices beyond the shores of the Maltese islands. I had to do something to meet this need. But how and what? How can I create a ripple effect? How can a study on some boys and literacy carried out in Malta empower others to adjust their expectations and behaviours in the fields of gender, literacy and early childhood within their respective contexts? The boys' voices needed a wider audience to know how their story in a postcolonial educational context goes, and figure out from its implications, the literacy curricula and early years education systems within their societies. This is how my idea transformed into a book.

When I look back, I realise that my lived experiences within Malta's particular sociocultural context, have played their part in shaping this book; as a child, a mother, an early childhood and primary school educator, a manager with the National Literacy Agency, an education officer (early years and quality assurance) and an academic. My voluntary positions as a co-founder and vice president of the Early Childhood Development Association of Malta (ECDAM), and a member of the board of administrators of the Malta Foundation for the Wellbeing of Society provide me with the opportunity to advocate for children's rights (United Nations, 1989) and quality early childhood education and care[1] (ECEC). These advocacy roles have also sustained my motivation and determined commitment to publish this book.

My late parents raised me with unconditional love and I shared most of my childhood with three brothers, up to the age of eleven, which is when my sister was born. From a young age, I was the voice of my illiterate father in his woodwork business. My brothers and sister were never keen on school, reading and writing. I was the first in my immediate family to graduate

Figure 0.1 My boys

with a master's and a doctoral degree. Having experienced how living as an illiterate and a literate individual influences the course of one's life generated a growing interest in the area of literacy from when I started my ECEC studies in 1997.

As a mother of two sons (see Figure 0.1) and having taught for some years in a boys' school during my journey as an educator, I experienced first-hand how some boys may become demotivated by school life and lifelong learning, particularly when they need to read or write. Conversely, as an educator, I also experienced how the realisation of theory in practice gives rise to effective and meaningful pedagogy that helps young boys flourish and become motivated readers and writers. This dissonance and a context of persistent global and local concern on boys' underachievement in literacy attainment sparked further interest to scrutinise the area of boys and early literacy in Maltese schools through my doctoral research. I wanted to discover more about how boys, from a young age, are experiencing reading and writing in school. What do several stakeholders and the young boys think about the way current literacy pedagogy is being promoted in a context where formal subject-based schooling starts at the age of five?

In my teaching career, I taught kindergarten for twelve years (working with three- to five-year-olds) followed by five years as a primary school teacher in a boys' school (working with five- to ten-year-olds; see Figure 0.2). Throughout this teaching journey, I realised how the knowledge

Figure 0.2 My years of teaching in a boys' primary school in Malta

acquired through my studies instilled in me a never-ending passion for the early years sector, and supported me as an educator – within schools and now university – to teach and learn with wonder, excitement and joy. I have witnessed how mandated curricula in the early primary years did not match the values and principles I honed regarding the ways in which young children learn best. Williams (2006) addresses the longstanding issue on who teachers are expected to be and who they are in their cultural contexts, stating that this conflict, 'has been felt by many teachers and teacher educators in Western societies, perhaps nowhere has it been felt more strongly than by educators in postcolonial societies around the world' (p. ix). I particularly felt what Williams (2006) is referring to here when I witnessed young children, in a postcolonial Maltese context, being pulled out of class to be tested for literacy at the age of five and teachers encouraged to promote a highly formalised approach to teach early reading and writing. I immediately felt that the effectiveness of such an approach within this context needed to be evaluated. Having developed a perception of young children as competent and able, I felt a growing need to uncover how reading and writing are being defined in schools through the participation of young boys who experienced a transition to formal schooling and literacy instruction at the age of five. As with other former British colonies, Malta has inherited a legacy of formal education which remains stubbornly in place even after almost sixty years of independence. Malta is one of a small number of countries in Europe where formal schooling starts in the scholastic year a child turns five (Ministry for Education and Employment, MEDE, 2013). This transition phase in a child's life is considered to be critical for the future of literacy attainment (Nutbrown, 2006; Roskos & Christie, 2007; Palmer & Bayley, 2013).

As I moved on to my role as a manager with the National Literacy Agency and an education officer within the Ministry for Education and Employment (Quality Assurance and Early Years) I continued to realise that the way literacy was being defined by several stakeholders in the broader Maltese educational context proved controversial. Surmounting promotion of the start of highly formalised early literacy instruction and literacy testing from the early years of schooling persists (DQSE, 2009). This push down of formal instruction contrasted with my understanding of how young children learn and it seemed to be jeopardising children's right to quality education and learning through play in early primary schooling. Such witnessed incongruity of theory and practice throughout my educational career and studies instilled in me a will to take action, deriving from a nurtured curiosity that longed for answers. Why does Malta have one of the widest gender gaps in literacy attainment, favouring girls? How is the present Maltese education system, that holds on to an inheritance of traditional and formal schooling from a young age, responding to such outcomes? Is the increasing pressure and exposure to highly formalised literacy instruction and one-size-fits-all literacy programmes at the age of five addressing this gender gap? What do stakeholders in education, especially young boys, have to say about literacy learning within such a schooling scenario? I was aware that there is no one solution to all this complexity, but these questions stirred up the will power needed to embark on a doctoral journey that investigated boys and early literacy learning in three Maltese state schools, and explored whether there are other ways that could make a difference. Yet, I strongly felt that the completion of this study was not the final chapter of my journey.

The early years sector has shifted from the position of the undervalued to one which is high on the agenda of national, European, and international policies with a determined quest to honour children's rights. Similarly, a global context of concern on boys' underachievement in literacy attainment top the education headlines to date, given that, on a global level, literacy is a human right. With many other reconceptualist and critical scholars (Cannella, 1997; Dahlberg et al., 2007, Lubeck, 1985; Soto & Swadener, 2002), I identify myself as an academic motivated by an everlasting passion and commitment to write with an intent to challenge universal ways and traditional approaches to early literacy education. In this book, I seek to challenge dominant ideologies that reproduce Euro-Western assumptions in early literacy curriculum and pedagogy through diverse stakeholders' perceptions, and young boys' views and experiences of learning to read and write in a postcolonial context. My intention is not to further promote existing gender binaries between boys' and girls' early literacy learning, but to create new understandings on the concept of boys' underachievement in literacy attainment and explore new possibilities in the way we look at gender, early literacy, and ECEC. I therefore present a case study focused on boys from a Maltese island state that embraces the advocacy potential of children's rights and postcolonial theory to raise awareness of more socially just ways of knowing, being, and doing (Cannella, 1997; MacNaughton, 2000) literacy in the early years. This book provides the reader with a learning opportunity to gain insights into the lived experiences of young boys within one particular postcolonial ECEC scenario. This book sets out to:

- Re-examine young boys' and stakeholders' perceptions on schooled early literacy through the advocacy potential of children's rights and postcolonial theory in a context where, like many other countries around the world, compulsory schooling and formal education start at the age of five.
- Offer practical recommendations for several stakeholders in education, at a local and global level, to challenge the norms in the fields of gender, literacy and ECEC for the under-sevens, and take action to produce a more pluriversal world to support all children in acquiring both academic and socially just goals.

Therefore, the overall aim of *Boys, Early Literacy and Children's Rights in a Postcolonial Context: A Case Study from Malta*, was not to publish a summary of my research study, but to retell the story of some young boys and several stakeholders through the potential advocacy of children's rights and the worldview of postcolonial theory. It is an attempt to confront Eurocentric and universal world orders that provide one-way routes of knowing gender, early literacy learning and ECEC for the under-sevens in Malta. Looking at the outcomes of this one Maltese case study from this fresh dual angle, this book brings us to the question: How do different stakeholders' perceptions, including young boys' views and experiences of early literacy learning within a postcolonial Maltese ECEC context, feature through the significant perspectives of children's rights and postcolonial theory?

Who is this book for?

This book has been written for educators (pre-service and in-service) who question complex and challenging literacy curricula and pedagogies grounded in colonialist legacies which are often a requirement to adopt in their classrooms. This book is also for those educators who strive to realise children's rights in a formal and traditional approach to education for the under-sevens and yearn to gain a deeper insight into the global discourse and research evidence on some boys' underachievement in literacy attainment. Additionally, this book should interest parents who want to learn more about boys' literacy and young children's rights and literacy experiences at school, as well as school leaders and policymakers who are cognisant of the enduring global concern and research evidence related to boys' literacy and need to inform their decisions and policies with evidence-based research that includes child participation. Finally, university students and academics who are interested in the fields of gender, early literacy, early childhood, children's rights and the impact of a colonial legacy on 21st-century ECEC, will find this book useful. Indeed, this book is an invitation to anyone who seeks to unsettle the taken for granted, and critically reflect and challenge longstanding narrow perceptions of looking at gender, literacy and early childhood.

Structure of the book

This book has been structured in five chapters. Each chapter leads to the next, though it is understandable that readers may prefer to focus more on some of the sections. For example, those interested in reading about what the young boys had to say about reading and writing may find Chapter 3 more appealing. At the end of each chapter, the reader is provided with five key takeaways that offer possible routes for rethinking and reconceptualising gender, literacy and ECEC in postcolonial contexts or other societies that embrace hierarchical gender binarism and a utilitarian approach to literacy and early education.

Overview of the book

Chapter 1 provides a background to the postcolonial context in which this book is situated – Malta. It also provides a rationale for positioning the dual lens of children's rights and postcolonial theory as a fresh perspective to re-examine the key findings of the presented case study. The chapter concludes by presenting the research design of the reported doctoral study concerning boys and early literacy learning in three Maltese state schools.

Chapter 2 focuses on how colonialist discourse in a postcolonial epoch structures our thinking, practice and relations. The colonial binary positioning of the colonising Self and the colonised Other is traced in gender stereotypes (favouring girls) and disguised duality in power relations within early literacy practices. Through the dual lens of children's rights and postcolonial theory, this chapter discusses and debates how the overlooked issue of gender may be negatively influencing the literate identities of some young boys in a Maltese ECEC context, and provides practical recommendations for present practice.

Chapter 3 shares the views of five- to six-year-old boys on the school reading and writing practices they experienced in three Maltese Year 1 classroms. The arguments build on the ways in which some boys got bored as they experienced an undesirable early literacy pedagogy. In other words, reading and writing practices in some schools are underpinned by dominant colonial ideologies and inequitable power relations. I argue that the definition of early literacy needs to be understood through the eyes of young children through sustained active child participation in policy, research and practice, to move towards more quality and inclusive early literacy pedagogies for all.

Chapter 4 highlights the need to rethink education for the under-sevens in settler colonial societies and how this may serve as a strategy to decolonise young children's and adult's minds from colonial legacies that settle in different shapes and forms within ECEC contexts. The data presented shows how the majority of the boys experienced low levels of involvement in learning, and points out a negative trend weaving through several stakeholders' claims in relation to play, early literacy and transitions in ECEC. The chapter concludes that a highly formalised approach to literacy for the under-sevens is not socially just and fails to honour the principles of children's rights in practice.

Chapter 5 provides an overview of the key takeaways and highlights implications for research and policy. To conclude, it uses the analogy of 'chartered waters' to close the circle of what this book set out to do. The analogy helps the reader to see how this book offers a critical reflective journey navigated through the advocacy potential of children's rights and postcolonial theory – an opportunity to refocus the lens and gain access to multiple ways of seeing and understanding boys, literacy and early childhood for the under-sevens.

In this book, the focus on boys is not based on the premise that girls cannot contribute to knowledge. I would like to highlight that the study presented in this book was not carried out with an intent to self-limit its approach to a racist or sexist methodology. Conversely, it aims to move away from gender binaries and rethink claims such as 'boys' underachievement' in an attempt to contribute to the fields of gender, literacy and ECEC at large. Scholarly work has revealed how some boys perform better than girls in literacy and how popular rhetoric and media are portraying *all* boys as lacking literacy competence.

In the same vein, I want to be extremely cautious about not generalising the arguments developed in this publication and providing a one-dimensional view of education in Malta. This book focuses on how early literacy pedagogy is experienced by five- to six-year-olds boys in three Maltese co-educational state schools. As with other postcolonial countries (Palmer, 2016), while subject-based teaching and compulsory schooling start at the age of five in Maltese schools, the findings presented are not representative of all early years education classrooms within church, independent and state schools in Malta. This study is constrained in its empirical investigation of boys' reading and writing experiences in three Maltese state schools in terms of generalisability. Yet, it offers a small-scale fresh diagnosis of valuable insights, and the outcomes are a valid contribution to the topic of inquiry, which has not yet been sufficiently unpacked. The next chapter digs into the past of the Maltese education system in an attempt to build the future. It presents the geographical, historical, theoretical, conceptual and methodological underpinnings of the reported case study concerning boys and early literacy in a postcolonial context.

Note

1 As defined in the General Comment (GC) No. 7 published by the United Nations (UN) Convention on the Rights of the Child, this paper uses the terms 'early childhood', 'early years' and 'early childhood education and care' to refer to 'the period below the age of 8 years.' (UN Committee on the Rights of the Child, 2005, p. 2).

References

Cannella, G. S. (1997). *Deconstructing early childhood education: Social justice and revolution.* Peter Lang.

Dahlberg, G., Moss, P., & Pence, A. (2007). *Beyond quality in early childhood education and care: Languages of evaluation.* Routledge.

Directorate for Quality and Standards in Education [DQSE]. (2009). *National policy and strategy for the attainment of core competences in primary education.* Ministry for Education, Culture, Youth and Sport. https://education.gov.mt/en/resources/Documents/Policy%20Documents/Attai%20Core_Competencies.pdf

Lubeck, S. (1985). *Sandbox society: Early education in black and white America.* Falmer Press.

MacNaughton, G. (2000). *Rethinking gender in early childhood education.* Allen & Ulwin.

Ministry for Education and Employment. (2013). *Early childhood education and care in Malta: The way forward.* https://education.gov.mt/en/Documents/Public%20Consultations/White%20Paper.pdf

Nutbrown, C. (2006). *Key concepts in early childhood education & care.* SAGE.

Palmer, S. (2016). *Upstart: The case for raising the school starting age and providing what the under-sevens really need.* Floris Books.

Palmer, S., & Bayley, R. (2013). *Foundations of literacy: A balanced approach to language, listening and literacy skills in the early years.* Featherstone.

Roskos, J. K., & Christie, J. S. (Eds.). (2007). *Play and literacy in early childhood: Research from multiple perspectives.* Routledge.

Soto, L. D., & Swadener, B. B. (2002). Toward liberatory early childhood theory, research and praxis: Decolonizing a field. *Contemporary Issues in Early Childhood, 3*(1), 38–66.

UN Committee on the Rights of the Child. (2005). *Implementing child rights in early childhood. general comment no. 7(CRC/C/GC/7/rev1, 2006).* Author. https://www2.ohchr.org/english/bodies/crc/docs/AdvanceVersions/GeneralComment7Rev1.pdf

United Nations. (1989). *Convention on the rights of the child.* https://www2.ohchr.org/english/bodies/crc/docs/AdvanceVersions/GeneralComment7Rev1.pdf

Williams, L. R. (2006). Foreword. In A. Gupta (Ed.), *Early childhood education, postcolonial theory, and teaching practices in India* (pp. vii–x). Palgrave Macmillan.

Acknowledgements

I start by thanking my two guardian angels, mum and dad, who never left my side while writing this book. I thank my better half, Joe, for the love, unwavering support and encouragement throughout this journey. I express my warmest gratitude to my two sons, Luc and Isaac. Our bond and your presence give me the right dose of daily energy to keep doing what I am most passionate about. A huge thanks go to my sister Sarita who used my late mother's magic touch to raise my spirits when needed. My young nephew and niece, Liam and Jade, thank you for the play and fun times together. These moments reminded me that no matter what, I needed to finish this book, as it is an act in the best interest of all children. And thank you brothers, spending most of my childhood years with three boys has also influenced my choice of studying boys and literacy.

I wish to acknowledge the inspiration and guidance of Professor Cathy Nutbrown, my doctoral supervisor in my work on boys' early literacy, and Professor Godfrey Baldacchino. Thanks to him, I was motivated to explore the field of postcolonial studies in this book. Professor Baldacchino, together with his wife Dr Anna Baldacchino, both friends and colleagues, wrote the foreword to this book – the cherry on the cake. A special thanks to both for your continued encouragement, help and support. When I was seventeen, I was lucky enough to meet the woman I call my 'mother in education', Mrs Grace Izzo, the one who instilled in me a lifelong passion for early years education. Words are not enough to thank you, Grace. I would also like to thank Professor Carmen Dalli and Professor Valerie Sollars, your valuable work in early childhood inspires me to keep going. I want to thank President Emeritus Marie-Louise Coleiro Preca, a leader whose work, dedication and commitment to children motivates me to continue advocating for the rights of every child.

I also want to recognise the help of Krista Bonniċi, whose attention to detail and aesthetic touch have made this book more inviting. In this regard, I also thank a special friend, Maria Saliba, whose comments and positivity were a blessing throughout this journey. Thanks also to all my family and friends, the Early Childhood Development Association of Malta (ECDAM) committee members, colleagues and the Early Childhood and Primary Education (ECPE) Research Group at the University of Malta for their relentless encouragement. A big thank you to Dr Rosienne Camilleri, for her empathy, words of support and for sending me an extract from Atwood's novella. She will be surprised to see how it ended up in the concluding chapter of this book. I extend my gratitude to a dear friend, Claire Mallia, who helped me provide quality images in this book.

I am also grateful to all the boys I met during my years of teaching and researching early and primary education in Malta. You inspired me to keep questioning whether all boys are being understood in their schooled literacy journeys right from the start, and I ultimately wrote my doctoral thesis and this book. Above all, I would like to thank all children, educators, families, colleagues and other stakeholders I met in my educational journey. This contribution to knowledge is the fruit of the experiences and learning I co-constructed with all of you.

I want to extend my sincere thanks for the financial support I received during my doctoral research. The Malta Government Scholarship Scheme has partly funded the presented study.

1 Boys and early literacy in a former British colony

The context and the study

Chapter Overview

The chapter provides the backdrop to the rest of the book. It is divided into two sections. The first presents the geographical, historical, theoretical and conceptual underpinnings that draw on a case study conducted in Maltese state schools. It sets off with an outline of the longstanding global and local concern on boys' literacy attainment. It then discusses the relevance of the geographical positioning and the precolonial, colonial, and postcolonial periods, and how it served as the feeder to contemporary political, social, economic and educational issues on the island. In view of this background, the chapter provides a rationale for adopting a book angle that integrates children's rights and postcolonial theory to confront and respond to the colonial legacies that surfaced in my doctoral work. The chapter explains how the identified fresh dual lens is used to re-examine the key findings of my doctoral study conducted in Malta to revitalise dialogue and discussion on the three concepts that frame this book: gender, early literacy learning and early childhood education and care (ECEC). The second section then presents the research design adopted for the doctoral study upon which this book is built. The chapter argues that this book may include one case study in a small island state but its lessons need to extend beyond Malta's limited shores. We need to understand our cultural legacy to influence who we become.

The context

Why boys and literacy in Malta?

The 'why' of gender differences in literacy achievement remains a popular question worldwide albeit with existing research evidence. I do not hold

DOI: 10.4324/9781003125525-1

the view that boys are underachievers and all girls are successful in literacy attainment. I witnessed the disengagement and demotivation as well as the joys, pleasures and successes of several boys' literate journeys throughout my teaching experience in Maltese schools. Beyond such experiences, I discovered a persistent international and national gender gap in literacy achievement favours girls (European Commision, 2017; Mifsud et al., 2000). For example, the Programme for International Student Assessment [PISA] (OECD, 2018) highlights a significant gap between girls' and boys' reading performance across participating countries. Malta has one of the largest gender gaps in literacy attainment and the highest percentages of early school leavers in Europe (Eurostat, 2020), both favouring females. Malta's government spending on education is above average in the European Union (EU). Yet, students' performance in international assessments related to science, reading and mathematics remain weak (Times of Malta, 2020). This means that Malta's return on investment in its education system is not apparent. Another gender issue in Malta and beyond its shores is suicide. It was recently reported that 88% of suicides in Malta account for men (The Malta Independent, 2018).

Scholarly work reveals a continued endeavour to understand gender differences in schooled literacy (Millard, 1997). Such work has been repeatedly criticised due to the tendency of positioning gender within binary constructs and the lack of focus on other factors which also influence literacy attainment, such as social class (MacNaughton, 2000; Weaver-Hightower, 2003). Yet, the evidence that some boys are more likely to underachieve in literacy remains (OECD, 2018) and this cannot be ignored. The issue with some boys and literacy performance has urged several education policymakers in different countries to prioritise the narrowing of the gender gap in literacy attainment within their national policy agendas. This includes Malta (MEDE, 2024). Boys' underachievement in literacy attainment, literacy pedagogy in ECEC and formal school starting age are never-ending debates in the global educational field. Thus, it is important to try to understand boys and literacy from the beginning of their journeys in a changing world, and within contexts that have diverse social, cultural, historical and political backgrounds. The following section seeks to speak of the past to portray a better understanding of the present Maltese education system.

The relevance of the precolonial, colonial and postcolonial periods to understand contemporary issues on gender, literacy and the early years in Malta

> You cannot understand our educational system, as you cannot understand many other things in Malta, without understanding the country's colonial and post-colonial contexts.
>
> Professor Peter Mayo (Maltatoday, 2012)

In an attempt to track down the origins of how some young boys came to experience early literacy in a certain manner, as my doctoral work revealed, I developed a growing interest to explore how this discovery may link to Malta's colonial past. This section considers the relevance of the geographical positioning and the precolonial, colonial and postcolonial periods, and how these things relate to contemporary political, social, economic and educational issues encountered in Malta.

The postcolonial small island state of Malta is geographically positioned in the middle of the Mediterranean Sea (see Figure 1.1). The islands comprise Malta, Gozo and Comino, and two unpopulated islands, Cominotto and Filfla. The main island is Malta, measuring 246 square kilometres (95 square miles). The population in Malta, in 2021, was 442,784 making it one of the most densely populated countries in the world. The official languages are Maltese and English, and 98% of Malta's inhabitants are Roman Catholic. The present education system in Malta comprises three sectors: state (60%), church (30%) and independent (10%). All state and most independent schools are co-educational. In the Maltese educational context, the terms 'early years', 'early childhood education', 'early childhood education and care' and 'early years cycle' refer to the phases in which infants and toddlers aged zero to three attend childcare, three – to five-year-olds attend kindergarten and five – to seven-year-olds join the first two years of compulsory formal schooling in primary schools, Years 1 and 2 (MEDE, 2012). The central geographical positioning of the Maltese islands in the Mediterranean Sea may have determined its destiny of a multilayered colonial period, which in turn makes the history of Maltese education quite particular and unique, yet similar to many other colonised countries in the world. Over time, Malta has sought to embrace an educational philosophy tied to the ideals and policies of its colonisers (Calleja, 1994).

Throughout its historical evolution, as with other countries around the globe, Malta has had multiple layers of cultural influences. The historical events presented and discussed in this next section provide a rationale for choosing to re-examine the findings of my doctoral work and look at them through a fresh perspective; one which partly zooms in through a postcolonial theoretical lens.

Malta's history goes back to the Arabs (870–1090 AD) who left a legacy on the language of the islanders living close to Europe, as Maltese is the only Semitic language written in Roman letters. Malta was also destined to be ruled by the Normans, Angevins, Swabians, Castilians and Aragonese through most of the Middle Ages. These Christian powers triggered the spread of formal education in Malta, as religious education was introduced and provided by members of the religious orders who acted as tutors to children of rich Maltese families (Laurenza, 1939). After the mid-1500s, under the Knights Hospitaller of St John, arts education thrived. Nevertheless, access to education amongst

Figure 1.1 Malta: A postcolonial small island state
Source: https://commons.wikimedia.org/wiki/File:Location_Malta_EU_Europe.png

the poor was extremely limited. All private schools were closed down under the short-lived French rule (1798–1800), and an attempt was made to introduce elementary education and some form of adult education.

In 1800, Britain took over Malta (see Figure 1.2) and set the stage for over 150 years of colonising the Maltese islands. Malta formally became a British crown colony in 1814. This makes it hard for Malta not to have some overtones of the British influence in its past (see Figure 1.3) and present education system. In her work on the history of early years education in Malta, Sollars (2018), mentions that, the:

> Instruction in Government elementary schools was formalised in April 1899 (NAM, Education Circulars 1861–1899). The subjects for the Infant and Preparatory class included Maltese, Arithmetic, weekly Object Lessons; Writing; Religious Instruction; Calisthenics; Needlework (for girls) and optional drawing (Kindergarten drawing)... Infants were admitted to the elementary school at the age of five. Infants

Figure 1.2 *The Bone of Contention or The English Bulldog and the Corsican Monkey* (implying Napoleon) by Charles Williams (1797–1830) published by S.W. Fores (London) on June 14, 1803. 'The image also refers to Britain's refusal to surrender Malta' (Times of Malta, 2021, p. 1)

Source: https://commons.wikimedia.org/wiki/File:The_Bone_of_Contention_or_the_English_Bull_Dog_and_the_Corsican_Monkey_MET_DP818517.jpg

'were organised in two classes: Stage 1 and Stage 2 and followed a pedagogy, notably arithmetic and reading (Ref Circular 3rd July 1915 – Scheme for teaching arithmetic)'. Maltese lessons were focused on the alphabet and an introduction to reading) . . . Writing (strokes and easy letters; round hand, on board and slates).

(pp. 341, 346)

This evidence reveals how five-year-olds were already exposed to highly-formalised early literacy instruction at the elementary school. Sollars (2018, p. 339) describes how Pullicino, director of education in colonial times (1850), advocated for 'infant schools for 2–6-year-old children to 'educate the heart', inculcate virtues and offer a pious upbringing besides general instruction and skills matching their 'tender abilities' (Pullicino 1850, p. 10).' Yet, almost thirty years after, 'Keenan (1879) reports seeing 'infants huddled together in a small stifling room' (p. 5)... where 'children are seated

Figure 1.3 Sr Connie Farrugia teaching the infants at St Joan Antide School, Gudja, Malta, in the late 1970s

Source: Times of Malta (2018, p. 1)

throughout the entire school day' (ibid. p. 8).' (Sollars, 2018, p. 339). A similar formal sedentary approach through subject-based teaching and learning and prioritising the conventional aspects of reading and writing for five-year-olds is prevalent to date (Bonello, 2021).

A rise in attention to Maltese culture and society on the islands was experienced when Malta became independent, stirring a quest for a Maltese philosophy of education (Calleja, 1994). Malta became a republic in 1974, dissolving allegiance with Britain after the Labour Party win in 1971. Independence brought symbolic freedom from British rule. At the same time however, it engendered a new model of domination, internationally referred to as neocolonialism or postcolonialism. Nkrumah (1965) defines neocolonialism as sustained economic, political, linguistic and cultural control exercised by colonisers over the colonised following the independence of a country. The birth of neocolonialism led to the evolution of neoliberalism, a system where imperialism – originating from the West – stubbornly perseveres. Neoliberalism and neocolonialism are byproducts or disguised forms of colonialism. Neoliberalism is linked to a free market system supporting private entrepreneurship and competition (Monbiot, 2017), and American linguist Noam Chomsky labels it the rival of democracy (Chomsky, 2016). Such a business model emanating from neoliberal policies impacts education systems and the wellbeing and performance of various ECEC stakeholders (Rogers et al., 2020; Hunkin, 2018). These are education systems that, at the political level, were perhaps meant to prioritise emancipation and social justice within postcolonial times. For example, a market approach to 21st-century Maltese ECEC is evident in the Free Childcare Scheme implemented with the intent to increase the participation of women in the labour market, diverting the focus from children's rights and needs, and moving forward towards high-quality and socially just ECEC.

This hidden colonial control surfaces in the ways the present education system in Malta promotes and assimilates the language, cultural, and educational philosophies of a British education model while demeaning its own. For example, when it comes to language, people in high positions still tend to use English to assert superiority and distance themselves from the lower class. Some 21st-century schools in Malta still prefer to use English as the first language – the language of power – and this is on the increase due to an influx of multiculturalism within schools. Such dualisms are also evident where individuals raised in English-speaking families in Malta may also be alienated by other groups who speak the native language. Colonisation is not just about its immediate influence, but also its long-term effects on people's lives including the ways they thought and acted in colonial and postcolonial times and how they think and act today. Similarly, the field of gender is influenced by a Euro-Western ideology that humans can be marginalised, creating legacies that continue to promote divisions between groups of people.

Nevertheless, in the 1988 the state was recognised as the body that controls the educational system and not the Minister of Education. This was a win for democracy in Maltese education. The Education Act of 1988, underpinned by the principles of democracy and lifelong education, was an intentional departure from a colonial education model and was seen as attempt to construct a Maltese education philosophy. However, it is interesting to note that in the same act, some decisions were still rooted in the past, such as the compulsory formal schooling, starting at age five. Only 12% of countries across the globe implement this approach to date and these have connections to colonial legacies (Palmer, 2016). Calleja (1994) raises the question as to whether educational acts in postcolonial times have led to a new education philosophy for Malta or a never-ending quest where the said philosophy is still in the making. Colonialism moved Maltese citizens to embrace foreign values, traditions and norms, and this created a long-term movement towards crafting a Maltese identity and education philosophy. It is well-documented that Malta's educational and examination systems are influenced by the British model (Cutajar, 2007; Sultana, 1997; Zammit Ciantar, 1993; Zammit Mangion, 1992).

The first National Minimum Curriculum (NMC) for Malta underpinned by a student-centred, emancipatory and lifelong learning perspective became law in 2000. The review of a National Curriculum Framework (NCF), grounded in the work of the National Minimum Curriculum (MEDE, 1999), started in 2009 and by 2012 it became law. This became the first national curriculum after Malta joined the European Union in 2004. In 2015, the NCF was supported by the proposed learning outcomes framework (MEDE, 2012) aimed to guide learning and assessment, and address the needs of all learners through increased curricula, colleges, schools, and learner autonomy as they are gradually freed from centrally imposed, knowledge-centric syllabi. Such policy documents show Malta's ongoing efforts to move towards democracy in education within a postcolonial epoch. Yet, research in actual practice shows that the education system is still hanging on to a legacy of the traditional philosophy of education (Baldacchino, 2018; Bonello, 2019), also through the present COVID-19 times (Bonello et al., 2021). To date, as with other colonised countries around the world, this has led to top-down curricula which transpired into 'schoolification' within ECEC practice (Sims, 2017; Woodhead & Moss, 2007). In her work on neoliberalism and ECEC, Sims (2017, p. 1) argues that educators have a key role in resisting the impacts of neoliberalism, as they can 'teach children to think critically', and that neoliberalism 'has a devastating impact on the early childhood sector with its focus on standardisation, push-down curriculum and its positioning of children as investments for future economic productivity'.

In several countries, like Malta, schoolification and formal instruction for young children persists through neoliberal thinking, policies, and early years practice (Nxumalo & Adair, 2018). For example, the work of Baldacchino (2018) uncovers the lingering effect of colonialism in the early years sector of two postcolonial small island states – Malta and Grenada. The influence of the British educational model was particularly present in:

> the preference for school uniforms; the widespread use of standard English as the language of instruction; a top-down, exam-driven pedagogy that obliges an early start to schooling; and a strong focus on literacy and numeracy in the early years. There are also restrictions in play-based learning; and story books, weather and alphabet charts that are not necessarily relevant to the country's culture and tradition and written in the English language, even though Malta and Grenada have their own vernacular.
>
> (p. iii)

More evidence of the inherited academic push down in a Maltese ECEC context can be traced in statements deriving from 21st-century early years policy documents, such as 'Once children are admitted to formal education, school becomes a very serious matter, even at the age of 5 and 6', and 'Rather than learning through play . . . children in classrooms are formally taught mostly factual information' (MEDE, 2006, p. 39).

The preparation of children for the labour market has brought about an alarming focus on literacy and numeracy in early years settings (Sims, 2017). This pressure is similarly evident in the *National Policy and Strategy for the Attainment of Core Competences in Primary Education* (DQSE, 2009), documented to ensure the mastery of three core competences in the education system: bilingual literacy, eliteracy and numeracy in the first years of compulsory schooling. In this document, the Maltese and English Core Competences Checklists 1, 2 and 3 were made available to teachers and schools in Malta (DQSE, 2009) as a guide for literacy instruction and to identify children, as from the age of five, who are not progressing satisfactorily in their Maltese and English literacy skills. After this summative assessment is carried out, the identified children would then be referred to start attending remedial literacy support which is locally referred to as 'complementary' sessions. The core competences checklists are grounded in the work of cognitive psychologists, such as Ehri (1995), where a universal and linear model to the skills, knowledge and understanding for reading and writing are introduced to children at particular ages. These early years teaching and learning processes are not in line with the NMC (MEDE, 1999) and the legislated NCF (MEDE, 2012). Both policy documents highlight that the first two years of compulsory schooling in Malta (five to seven years) 'must be regarded as the formative period which precedes the one during which the school experience becomes more formal' (p. 57).

Such incoherent early years policies, persistent neoliberal barriers and challenges intrigued me to explore how these underlying tensions are impacting early literacy pedagogy and boys in postcolonial Malta. The way early literacy learning is approached in schools seems to be reinforcing the inequities of domination. Contemporary literacy assessment models and resources used to teach languages to under-sevens tend to conform educators and children and this is why I am interested in the concept of decolonisation when it comes to gender, literacy and early childhood education and care. This evidence indicates that despite over 60 years of independence, the Maltese education system, as with other countries (Barongo-Muweke, 2016), is not decolonised yet.

With Walter Mignolo (2011, p. xxvii). this book understands decolonisation as a praxis that demands 'thinking and doing'. As Wright puts it: 'Clearly, then, decolonisation can be said to be an articulation of diverse progressive thinkers and projects from (former?) colonies around the world' (p. 25). Popular terms in literature such as 'decolonising education' (McGregor & Marker, 2018) and 'decolonising literacy' (Wolstein, 2017) are used in an attempt to criticise and question colonisers perceptions of what counts as knowledge and literacy. This entails who makes decisions on how learning occurs and the dominance of Western education over a myriad of nations. Papen (2005) stated that to decolonise literacy education a country requires researchers and programme creators that seek to uncover the lived everyday experiences, power relationships, discourses and practices around literacy. The deployment of decolonisation within traditional (i.e., Eurocentric, universal and hegemonic) perspectives features prominently within the developed key arguments that chapters of this book provide. This book explores how decolonisation can be applied to the fields of gender, early literacy learning and ECEC within a Maltese postcolonial small island state context. The fors and againsts related to the impact of colonisation on the Maltese islands are fodder for a never-ending dispute; essentially a 'double-edged sword' (Maltatoday, 2012). On the one hand, the period (almost 200 years) under British rule was crucial for the modernisation and development of Malta. For example, the creation of jobs, the introduction of trade unionism and the learning of the English language. On the other hand, colonisation also had its negative effects on Malta. How the colonisers viewed the world was gradually and consistently imposed on the colonised. Western education was embedded with enthusiasm given the bright future it promised for Maltese citizens. Teaching and learning during colonialism were grounded in rote learning and memorisation, creating a barrier to possibility, creative and critical thinking (Kano, 2006). Some still try to protect this educational philosophy, one that overlooks anything that leads to thinking and imagination or desires. Colonial education indoctrinated the vision of the colonised making them submissive to the colonisers (Bacchus, 2006; Kano, 2006).

In light of the geographical and historical background presented above, this book explores the potential of postcolonial theory to revitalise dialogue and discussions and unsettle normalising discourse that engenders inequities in the fields of gender, early literacy learning and ECEC.

Adopting a postcolonial theoretical lens

Postcolonial theory receives attention from the education field because it re-examines the role of colonial education on the identity and cultures of ex-colonised countries (Viruru, 2005). As specified in the work of Viruru (2005) the purpose of postcolonialism is 'addressing the legacy of colonialism imposed by western attempts to dominate the globe over hundreds of years' (p. 8). The author continues to argue how postcolonialism is a form of hope to many countries seeking to think of new possibilities and to be freed from Western domination. Loomba (1998, p. 12) does not view postcolonialism as a period in history that comes after colonialism 'but also as the contestation of colonial domination and the legacies of colonialism'. Said (2003), through his work on Orientalism, points out the superiority of the West over the 'others', while Bhabha (2004) highlights the engendered 'hybridity' underpinning the tension between the cultures of the colonisers and the colonised. Such definitions portray postcolonial theory as an academic discourse that seeks to unpack the legacies of British rule and its impact on past and present political, social, cultural and economic lives of human beings in diverse countries, including small island states. As specified in the work of Baldacchino (2010, p. 193):

> small islands have taken the longest to consider independence (Doumenge, 1985), they have also been – with the exception of the Pacific – among the earliest territories to be colonized, so retaining colonial links for longest.
>
> (Caldwell et al., 1980)

Despite the impact of colonialism on ECEC in several countries, including the early years education sector on the small island state of Malta (Baldacchino, 2018), postcolonial theory does not feature prominently in the academic discipline of ECEC (Viruru, 2005). Bloch (1992) points out that the dominance of science education grounded in developmental psychology and Euro-Western ideologies has marginalised other essential perspectives from the field of ECEC (e.g., postcolonial and feminist). This universalism has been interrogated by several reconceptualist scholars (Bloch, 1992; Cannella, 1997; Lubeck, 1985). Some research studies applied postcolonial theory in diverse ways (Baldacchino, 2018; Gupta, 2013; Kaomea, 2003; Viruru, 2005). Such studies challenge dominant views of traditional Western education and childhood with more socially just ways of being and knowing. Repeatedly, research shows that effective practice in early years education does not embrace the Western dominant and traditional understanding of children and childhood (Pence, 2011, Viruru, 2005). Yet, postcolonial theory has been criticised for its focus on rejecting Western ideologies and supremacy, the use of an ambiguous term 'post' as a reference to an end to colonialism, and the notion of being too general as a theory and old-fashioned. With Said (2003), I agree that postcolonial theory should not be used to promote binaries between colonial and postcolonial times or merely seek to focus on dominance or rejection of history.

During my doctoral journey, I did not consider the study as functioning through a postcolonial framework, yet the aftermath led to its adoption. I adopt a postcolonial perspective to re-examine the way five-to six-year-old boys were perceived when it comes to early literacy learning and how they experienced schooled reading and writing practices in a Maltese postcolonial ECEC context. Thus, through this lens, this book unveils the tensions and hybridity between the educational philosophies underpinning a progressive philosophy of education and the educational philosophy of the British colonisers. It is not my intention to create further binaries between the different educational philosophies, but instead I aim to contextualise these ideas to create a deeper understanding of how these have shaped the ideas on gender and literacy pedagogies within the present socioculturally constructed ECEC system and early literacy curriculum in Malta. There is a need to understand the different dynamics (historical, political, cultural, etc.) that have sculpted today's ECEC system and early literacy education in Malta. The work presented in this book is a contribution to this identified gap in knowledge.

Postcolonial theory offers the highly contested topic on boys underachievement in literacy attainment a viewpoint of critique that reveals diverse journeys and meanings of gender, literacy and early years education embedded in discourse within unconscious cultures and contexts. On a macro-sociocultural level, it also offers the concerned topic a theoretical lens to critique the longstanding legacy of Eurocentrism evident in the colonial practices and existing traditional literacy approaches, to better understand its influence and impact on gender and education within postcolonial states. Ultimately, in this book postcolonial theory is significant as an analytical tool of the reported study because it transpires an uninformed and persistent colonial impact on the Maltese education system, and broadens the conceptualisation of the disciplines of gender, literacy and early years education for advancement. Macedo (1999) believes that 'our minds, if not our hearts will remain colonised' if postcolonial theory is overlooked in educational research, limiting society from a deeper understanding of its continued legacy (p. xv).

Collapsing the boundaries: confronting colonialist legacies in literacy and early years education through the advocacy potential of children's rights and postcolonial theory

> One of the major challenges that early childhood scholars and educators in (post) colonial settler societies now face is the question of how best to confront and respond to these colonialist legacies and challenges in their work with young children.
>
> (Pacini-Ketchabaw & Taylor, 2015, p. 19)

The statement above mirrors a persistent challenge in my different roles within a postcolonial Maltese education sector. The year 1989 brought about a change in the way people perceive children and childhood following two world wars – where children were more seen rather than heard or respected as human beings. This change was triggered by the formal ratification of the United Nations Convention of the Rights of the

Child (UNCRC), to recognise children (0–18 years) with welfare and citizenship rights, in most of the countries worldwide. The inculcation of a Western philosophy of education is a jeopardy to the ideology underpinning the most ratified world treaty in history, children's rights. Sartre (2005) claims that colonialism deprives human beings of their rights. As evident in the previous sections, the Maltese society may have grown up hesitant to stand up for its rights, sober to injustice and alienated from its traditions, culture and heritage. Past my doctoral work, one argument emerged out of the analytics and became something on which I wanted to build more. This argument identifies a gap between the principles underpinning the most ratified world treaty, the UNCRC, and its mission to honour these rights in practice. It helped me to locate the book angle that served my purpose (together with a postcolonial lens) and determine a wider audience due to its advocacy potential. Scholarly literature convinced me that children's rights can be a major driver for policy change in the fields of gender, literacy and ECEC, as evident in the following two statements:

> Children's rights play an important role in policy developments in early childhood education (ECE) because they promote social justice and empowerment for children, highlight the impact of early childhood experiences and question traditional assumptions about the competence and agency of young children.
>
> (Smith, 2017, p. 452)

> The International Reading Association declares that it is time to build reading programs on a set of comprehensive principles that honor children's rights to excellent reading instruction.
>
> (International Reading Association, n.d., p. 1)

Like many other countries, Malta ratified the UNCRC over 30 years ago and is one of the 27 small island states in the world, 20 of which were colonised by Britain (Baldacchino, 2018). The Convention has 54 articles underpinned by three main categories: provision rights, protection rights and participation rights. The Maltese National Children's Policy (Ministry for the Family, Children's Rights and Social Solidarity, 2017), 'grounded in a person-centred life-course approach' (p. 14) promotes the realisation of these three key principles of children's rights in the lives of children.

Countries who ratified this Convention are obliged to comply and safeguard these rights through the required action. A Convention is more mandatory than the preceding two declarations – Geneva Declaration of 1924 and Declaration of the Rights of the Child of 1959. Both declarations and the 1979 UN International Year of the Child influenced the course towards envisioning children's rights as a serious matter. Tobin (2011, as cited in Smith, 2017) points out that 'rights provide the lens by which all impact on children should be reviewed and resolved' (p. 88). Such powerful statements, and the key findings of my doctoral work, further stimulated my interest in working on a book that confronts and responds to how colonialist legacies impact some young boys and early literacy learning in Malta through a postcolonial and child's rights perspective.

The interdisciplinary theoretical framework of this book brings together two worldviews that tend to be handled separately. As pointed out in the work of Viruru (2005), postcolonial theory, on the one hand, is used to combat oppression associated with a denial of freedom. On the other hand, Viruru also argues that children's rights, a form of universal law, would not feature in a postcolonial scholar's portfolio because universal rights may be regarded as an invisible form of oppression or 'civilized oppression' (Harvey, 1999, p. 1, as cited in Viruru, 2005). Yet, advocates for children's rights (Alderson, 2004; Hart, 1997; Smith, 2017) perceive the UNCRC as a tool for advocacy potential in terms of shifting the balance of power for children to exercise agency. Thus, I argue that the Convention, if regarded from a more nuanced perspective for the betterment of today's complex world, may be viewed as a tool that can join forces with postcolonial theory to confront oppression and support the notions of freedom, rationality and equality – rather than perceived as a simplistic form of universal law. Through a conscious effort to navigate through and respond to the colonialist legacies that surfaced as I unpacked the three concepts that frame this book, gender, literacy and ECEC, I decided to adopt the dual lens of children's rights and postcolonial theory (see Figure 1.4).

The work of Seremani and Clegg (2015) builds on Bhabha's notion of 'third space', challenging dualisms and introducing the idea of 'epistemological third spaces'. They argue that diverse perspectives may coexist, and are negotiated and renegotiated through dialogue over a period of time (Bhabha, 2004). It is a space where progression overcomes dichotomy and where cultures overlap. Embracing this philosophical element of hybridity, this book collapses the boundary between the universal and pluriversal worldviews of postcolonial and child's rights theories. Thus, an epistemological third space allowed me, as Seremani and Clegg (2015) put it: 'to portray the complex and ambivalent realities of different settings better, settings that are often hybrids of intermingled worldviews' (p. 6).

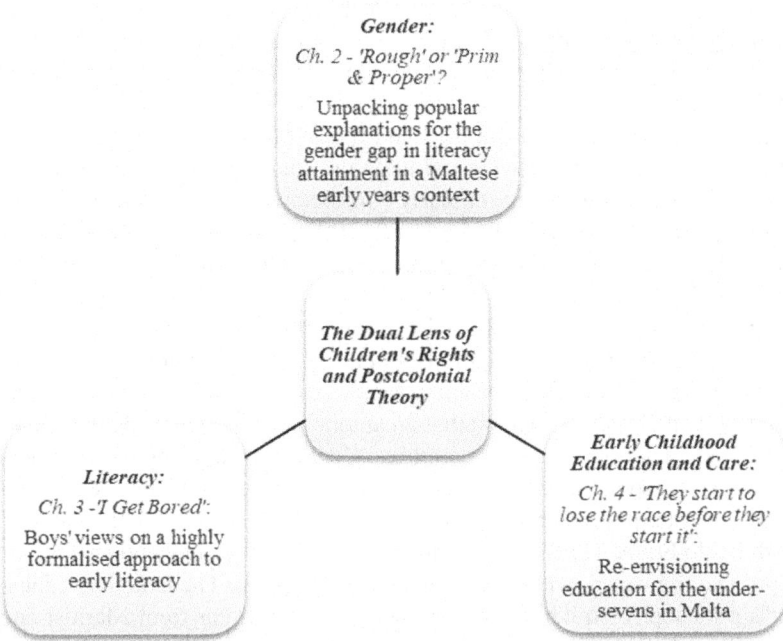

Figure 1.4 The theoretical and conceptual underpinnings that frame the three key arguments presented in this book

Theoretical models of literacy, child's rights discourse and postcolonial educational contexts

This section provides a brief overview of the evolution of literacy across time to provide a contextual background for boys' early literacy in postcolonial Malta and analyses how this fits in child's rights discourse. The relationship between Western education, language and literacy cannot go unnoticed:

> Throughout most of the nineteenth and twentieth centuries, the teaching of reading (certainly in Western countries and their sponsored campaigns elsewhere), commonly focused heavily on the explicit coaching of skills in sound-letter relationships.
>
> (The Open University, n.d., p. 1)

The expansion of formal schooling in 20th-century Malta provided the possibility for several individuals to become literate. How being 'literate' was interpreted at the time is different from the broader view of 'literacy' in 21st-century literature. Literacy used to be associated with the ability to read and write, and individuals who were unable to do so were referred to as 'illiterate' (Roberts, 1995). Over time, the definition of literacy has shifted from literacy as skill or school knowledge to literacy as a sociocultural construct constantly being 'negotiated and renegotiated' (Alloway & Gilbert, 1997, p. 51). The latter is referred to as the social practice perspective of literacy prominent in recent scholarly work known as 'new literacy studies' (NLS) (Gee, 1991; Street, 2003). Street (1984) promotes the idea of multiple literacies and what it means by presenting the contrasting 'autonomous' and 'ideological' models of literacy.

The two models capture the shift in the definition and interpretation of literacy over time. The autonomous model represents the notion of literacy as the acquisition of skills needed to speak, read and write a language. Larson and Marsh (2015) contend that an autonomous model of literacy backs the curricula adopted in many countries. Conversely, the ideological model of literacy is socially constructed between individuals and shaped by economic, social, political and cultural contexts (Street, 1984). This is in line with Paulo Freire's (1970) perspective of literacy of reading and writing the word and the world, with reality as the starting point. The Brazilian educator's philosophy on education for liberation, stemming from Marxist and existentialist paradigms, 'has greatly influenced the approaches and models used in literacy learning' (Rugut & Osman, 2013, p. 23). Inspired by the work of Freire (1970) and the relevance of his ideas to literacy education in the early years, the chapters of this book draw on some of his philosophical concepts on education, including banking education, problem-posing model, conscientisation, codification, culture circle and praxis. For example, the conclusion of each chapter is framed within his concept of praxis – an invitation for the reader to develop praxis, a process of dialogue, reflection and action (or intervention) to create political change.

As an early childhood educator for almost two decades, I experienced several debates concerning the teaching of literacy. One of the persistent challenges, then and now, is how reading and writing – both recognised as literacy activities – should be taught in a 21st-century Maltese early years system. Never-ending debates among ECEC stakeholders in Maltese schools revolve around whether reading in Maltese and English (both official languages) should be taught through a phonics approach, a whole language approach, or both. Another longstanding dispute is whether early literacy learning, up till the age of seven, should be nurtured through play or taught through highly formalised literacy instruction or a balance of both. The presented work promotes the sociocultural view of literacy education. This perspective nurtures creativity and critical thinking through child-centred, inclusive and collaborative practices empowering children to make meaning of the varied literacy experiences they are exposed to in their education and lives. It can be distinguished from the transmission model, rote learning and memorisation promoted through education in colonial times (Kano, 2006) – a model rival to democratic practice (Chomsky, 2016) and a rights-based approach (United Nations, 1989) in education. This book provides a case study that seeks to gain a deeper insight into how such contrasting theoretical perspectives about literacy have been shaped through time in a Maltese postcolonial small island state. In times where children's rights are high on the ECEC policy agendas, what is being counted as literacy in a postcolonial ECEC context? Is literacy being promoted in 21st-century ECEC honouring children's rights in educational practice? In what ways did the power of the past shape the future of literacy for some boys in a Maltese state school context?

In sum, the first section of this chapter provided an overarching rationale as to how the advocacy potential of children's rights and postcolonial theory offer the topic of boys and early literacy a theoretical dual lens to support the case for:

- critiquing the longstanding legacy of colonial influence in literacy and early childhood education;
- advocating for the realisation of children's rights in literacy and early childhood education;
- researching literacy learning in a context where five- to six-year-old boys experience formal and subject-based schooling; and
- promoting an ideological model for 21st-century literacy in early childhood education.

The study

This section presents a summary of the research design chosen for my doctoral study (Bonello, 2018) upon which this book is centred. Following the adoption of the principles of a convergent parallel design in Mixed Methods Phenomenological Research (MMPR) (Creswell & Plano Clark, 2011) I sought to answer the research questions (Table 1.1) through (i) an online questionnaire sent to early primary educators, (ii) classroom observations, and (iii) by giving voice to fourteen five- to six-year-old boys, three Year 1 teachers (working with five- to six-year-olds), three heads of schools, three heads of department (literacy) and fourteen parents of boys in three Maltese state schools.

Data were collected between January and March of 2017. A pilot study was conducted in a fourth school before the start of data collection within the three state schools concerned. The pilot project consisted of three full

Table 1.1 Methods matrix underpinned by the principles adopted from a convergent parallel design in mixed methods

Question number	Research Questions: Three subsidiary research questions and one overarching research question	Methods
1	What is the relationship between the rhetoric on boys' underachievement (in media and educational research) and Maltese state school teachers' beliefs in, and practices of, boys and literacy in the early primary years?	Online questionnaire for classroom teachers and literacy teachers working in the early primary years of Maltese state schools
2	How are existing reading and writing practices within Maltese primary state schools impacting five- to six-year-old boys' involvement in literacy learning, and how are these consistent with current research on effective early literacy practices?	Observations of three state schools and three Year 1 classrooms (five- to six-year-old boys)
3	What are the views of teachers, heads of school, heads of department (literacy) and parents on boys' underachievement, and how do these stakeholders and young boys perceive existing reading and writing practices in the early primary years of a Maltese state school?	Interviews with heads of school, heads of department (literacy) and Year 1 teachers. Focus groups with parents and boys (five- to six-year-olds)
4	Overarching research question: Within the global context of concern on boys' underachievement, how are boys experiencing reading and writing in the early primary years of Maltese state schools?	Interpretation of the merged results will provide an answer to the overarching research question. Identify content areas, similarities and differences between all methods used for data collection in this study.

Source: Creswell & Plano Clark (2011)

school days of observation (18 hours of classroom observation). I conducted interviews with the head of school, the chosen Year 1 teacher and two focus groups with parents and boys. Together, the outcomes from the pilot study contributed to the process of reviewing the questions and reflecting on the approach to be used with the different participants of the main study.

The three Maltese state schools

I chose to conduct my enquiry in state schools since it is the sector that has the largest percentage of compulsory education provision in Malta, and consequently a higher percentage of children attend state schools (DQSE, 2015). Three from the sixty-seven primary state schools in the Maltese islands were chosen through convenience sampling. These schools were chosen to produce richer understandings of young boys' lived reading and writing experiences, and to represent educational settings situated in both the northern and southern geographical regions of the island, with different socioeconomic, cultural and linguistic backgrounds.

The research methods

Online questionnaire

The online questionnaire assisted in providing a richer picture and setting the general terrain of the phenomenon under investigation in a Maltese context. The questionnaire was adapted from the work of Alloway et al. (2002) on boys, literacy and schooling. The study by Alloway et al. (2002) inspired the roots of this enquiry since similar data from a Maltese context seemed to be lacking. The online questionnaire (developed through Google Forms) was sent out to 400 teachers in the early primary years of all Maltese state schools in 2017. The participants in this online survey were early primary classroom teachers (teaching five- to seven-year-olds), literacy support teachers (providing classroom teachers and complementary teachers with in-class and pull-out literacy support) and complementary teachers (providing literacy support to children from the age of five, mainly through pull-out and also in-class sessions). The purpose for selecting this particular group of participants was to include those teachers involved with the daily literacy pedagogies and practices during the first two years of compulsory schooling in Maltese state schools (Years 1 and 2 – five- to seven-year-olds). A total of 193 out of 400 participants (48%) responded to the two-minute online questionnaire. Likert scale items were underpinned by popular discourses in media and educational research related to the concepts of 'boys' underachievement', 'early literacy learning'. and 'school readiness'. The open-ended questions focused more on reading and writing practices. The validity and rigour of this questionnaire were taken into consideration through the piloting phase. For this book, parts of the quantitative data from this online questionnaire will be presented and triangulated with some of the key findings emerging from classroom observations, interviews and focus groups of the broader study.

Observations in three Year 1 classrooms (five- to six-year-olds)

Classroom observations were conducted for one week in each of the three schools to obtain a more comprehensive understanding of the boys' schooled reading and writing experiences. Following parental consent, observations provided me with the opportunity to collect live data from five- to six-year-old boys' schooled reading and writing experiences. This method enhanced the validity and authenticity of my findings, as the study did not rely solely on the second-hand accounts obtained from the online questionnaire, focus groups and interviews. I adopted the role of 'observer as participant' (Gold, 1958), the most ethical approach to observations, as the participants are informed by the researcher's activities and the researcher is more focused on collecting data rather than being involved in the activity to be observed. During the direct structured observation, I used two types of observation schedules that were collated in one prepared schedule (Bryman, 2016). I sought similarities and differences to capture the effect of the pedagogical styles on the level of boys' involvement during reading and writing practices through:

- direct observations in the form of a prepared structured observation schedule using narrative descriptions;
- the Leuven Scale of involvement in learning (Laevers, 1994) – five level descriptors (see Figure 1.5) – to measure the level of boys' involvement in each of the reading and/or writing practices observed. The level of involvement in learning was rated between levels one to five, one being the lowest.

Underpinned by experiential education (EXE) theory, the descriptors allowed for obtaining data through non-verbal behaviour. In the context of this enquiry, an early question was: How was I going to find out what counts as quality reading and writing practices from boys' perspectives? While well-being and involvement are two crucial factors that determine a good school (Laevers, 1994), my study focused on the second criterion of involvement of young boys during their reading and writing practices to provide the required answers to the research questions. Involvement is

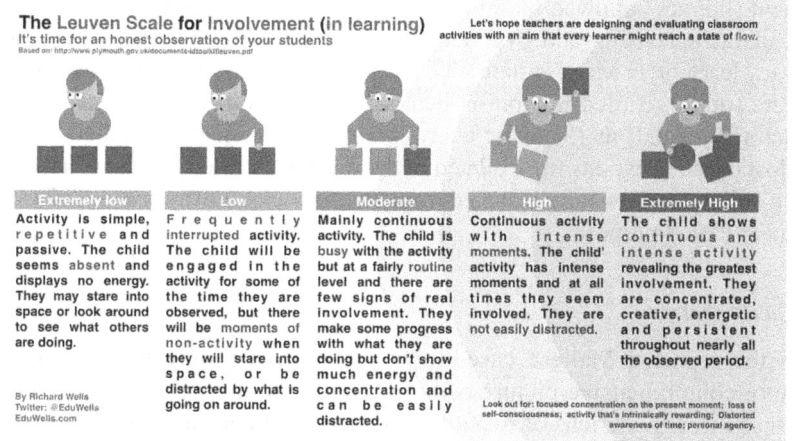

Figure 1.5 The Leuven Scale of involvement in learning: Five level descriptors (Laevers, 1994). Image created by Richard Wells. EduWells.com

Source: https://eduwells.com/2015/02/28/can-ipads-help-achieve-a-state-of-flow/

central to EXE theory; the quality dimension of the criterion of involvement in learning is the exploratory drive, or 'the need to get a better grip on reality, the intrinsic interest in how things and people are and why reality is like it is' (Laevers, 1994, p. 163).

In each school, ratings from the five consecutive days of observing boys' level of involvement in learning during reading and writing practices were then analysed by manual counting and then entered into Excel bar graphs. At the same time, narrative data collected from the prepared observations schedules were filed and a snapshot of the recorded scenarios are presented in this book. Research shows that the combination of both quantitative and qualitative data for classroom observations take a more comprehensive picture of what happens in classrooms (Bryman, 2016). Lastly, the time that I spent doing classroom observations (one week with approximately 25 hours of observation in each school) provided me with 'thick descriptions' of the lived experiences, and as a result, the collected data was 'strong on reality' (Cohen et al., 2007, p. 405).

Semi-structured interviews

After the observation phase, face-to-face interviews with three Year 1 teachers (teaching five- to six-year-olds – the same teachers that participated in the classroom observations), three heads of school and three heads of department (literacy) allowed for an in-depth exploration of their perceptions on 'underachievement' and lived experiences concerning boys and early literacy learning in Maltese state schools. The nine semi-structured interviews were audio-recorded and transcribed verbatim to facilitate the procedure of qualitative analysis (thematic analysis) and to minimise researchers' bias. Most of the questions were related to the open and closed questions used in the online questionnaire (adapted from the study of Alloway et al., 2002) for triangulation purposes.

Focus groups

In the reported Maltese case study, focus groups were used to get a more comprehensive picture of boys' lived reading and writing experiences through the lens of two different groups of participants. Two focus groups were conducted in each school setting; one with five- to six-year-old boys and another with the parents of boys from the chosen Year 1 classroom.

Parents' focus groups

The rationale for the parents' focus groups in this enquiry was to evaluate different views from the parents of the five- to six-year-old boys, gather in-depth explanations and to create further understandings of their sons' experiences. Focus groups were particularly chosen to make it easy and more comfortable for parents to speak up on this topic. Three groups of parents were chosen through purposive sampling. All the parents of boys in each of the three classrooms (eight to ten maximum) were invited and the number of consent forms returned was counted before confirmation. In my study, two groups of five parents and one group of four parents returned their respective consent forms and agreed to participate.

Throughout the collection of this data, I took on the role of a moderator in a focused discussion on the phenomenon of this enquiry. The three focus group discussions were audio-recorded. All recordings (English, Maltese and Italian languages were used during one of the parents' focus groups; Maltese was used in the other two) were transcribed verbatim in English (for audience purposes) and a thematic analysis approach was used to analyse the transcript data. To avoid inconveniencing parents, all three focus groups were conducted 45 minutes before the end of the school day so they would be able to collect their sons after the focus group interview ended.

Boys' focus groups

My doctoral research stance was committed to listening to the voices of five- to six-year-old boys through three separate focus groups. Each focus group was conducted in one of the three Maltese state schools chosen for the reported case study. The fourteen boys were chosen through purposive sampling. The boys' parents received an information letter requesting parental informed consent for their sons to participate in the study and ensure anonymity and confidentiality. Given that young boys are vulnerable participants, their oral consent was obtained through an informal conversational question-and-answer procedure. This process was witnessed by one adult who was employed in the same school. A child-friendly booklet was prepared for this oral consent. The boys made a thumbprint (as a nose) in a smiley face if they consented to participate or in a sad face if otherwise.

The five- to six-year-old boys were in Year 1 (their first year of compulsory schooling and subject-based lessons) following two years of kindergarten (three- to five-year-olds). During the one week of observation in each school, I used photography to capture the reading and writing practices experienced by the boys. The pictures served as a visual tool and operated as mediational means in talking and listening during the three focus groups. The photo-mediated oral consultations offered a space for the boys to express their views on the schooled reading and writing practices they experienced. The participation of the boys in this case study was presented to them as a right (Nutbrown, 1996; United Nations, 1989) to safeguard this study from being categorised as an inquiry where young children are silenced. During the focus groups, I took on the role of a 'discussion facilitator' (Robert-Holmes, 2005, p. 13), as I was particularly interested in ways the boys could respond to each other's opinions rather than as individuals. I wanted to shift the power dynamics of the conversation in their favour (Brooker, 2001) and make them feel less intimidated than in an adult-to-child dialogue (Cohen et al., 2007). Conscious of the potential risk of having the boys re-voicing each other, I used child-friendly engagement methods. I was prepared to modify the questions whenever needed to assist them in expressing their thoughts, feelings and as well to encourage more detailed responses.

Each focus group was presented as a short conversation, more like a group circle time in a room the boys were already familiar with within their school (Shaw et al., 2011). I conducted the focus group with the boys on the last day of one week of observations, giving them time to familiarise themselves with me and also feel comfortable to speak up in my presence (Barley & Bath, 2014). The photographs helped in making the focus group interviews more cooperative. Together, we revisited and reviewed the read-ing and writing moments captured with the camera. The visual images ena-bled the boys to think and act as agents of their learning. Each boy was provided with a kid-friendly emotion card with three small faces (happy, neutral and sad). I described how they were going to be shown a picture of themselves during their classroom activities on a tablet device and that they could point at one of the faces on their cards to show how they felt and maybe add anything else they would like to say about that photograph. This child-friendly strategy kept the boys active, as when they looked at the image on the tablet they pointed at one of the faces and traced the mouth of the face they chose with their fingers. It also helped in making them express how they felt at that particular point in time.

The data from the focus groups, together with other stakeholders' interviews in the broader study, were analysed through thematic analy-sis (Braun & Clarke, 2006). The computer software programme NVivo 11 was used for categorising, coding and data storage. The emergent patterns and themes served as a sound basis for the presentation of the key findings. The process of data reduction through thematic analysis and NVivo 11 was chosen to minimise the possibility of researchers' bias. Given that five- to six-year-old boys' ability to be honest might be doubted, the validity of this data might be cautioned. In this light, I was mindful of the fact that children's views on literacy are shaped by various elements, including context, time and space, and thus the triangulation of the overall data through multiple methods, the reported study addressed potential issues of data collection, data analysis and interpretation to minimise any validity and credibility threats. The boys' views were tran-scribed verbatim without any filter. Their opinions offer an authentic insight into the young boys' school reading and writing experiences in a Maltese postcolonial context.

This chapter provided an overview of the geographical, historical, theo-retical and conceptual underpinnings that frame this book. A rationale for the set boundaries raises the case for re-examining the key findings of my doctoral study through the dual lens of children's rights and postcolo-nial theory. The second section presented the research design adopted for the reported case study. It is hoped that the presented research process is adapted by others, particularly those who are interested in having young children participate in their research. The next three chapters highlight the three key arguments that emerged from a re-examination of the key find-ings. This book is based on one case study in a small island state, but the statistical data and power of stakeholders' voices may inform present edu-cational outcomes through a needed connection with a cultural-historical colonial background in Malta and beyond.

References

Alderson, P. (2004). Ethics. In S. Fraser, S. Lewis, S. Ding, M. Kellet & C. Robinson (Eds.), *Doing research with children and young people* (pp. 97–112). London: Sage.

Alloway, N., Freebody, P., Gilber, P., & Muspratt, S. (2002). *Boys, literacy and schooling: Expanding the repertoires of practice*. J.S. McMillan Printing Group.

Alloway, N., & Gilbert, P. (1997). Boys and literacy: Lessons from Australia. *Gender and Education, 9*(1), 49–60.

Bacchus, M. K. (2006). The impact of globalization on curriculum development in postcolonial societies. In Y. Kanu (Ed.), *Curriculum as cultural practice: Postcolonial imaginations* (pp. 260–279). University of Toronto Press.

Baldacchino, A. (2018). *Early childhood education in small island states: A very British story* (PhD thesis). University of Sheffield.

Baldacchino, G. (2010). "Upside down decolonization" in subnational island jurisdictions: Questioning the "post" in postcolonialism. *Space and Culture, 13*(2), 188–202. https://doi.org/10.1177/1206331209360865.

Barley, R., & Bath, C. (2014). The importance of familiarisation when doing research with young children. *Ethnography and Education, 9*(2), 182–195.

Barongo-Muweke, N. (2016). *Decolonizing education: Towards reconstructing a theory of citizenship education for postcolonial Africa*. Springer.

Bhaba, H. (1994). *The location of culture*. Routledge.

Bloch, M. (1992). Critical perspectives on the historical relationship between child development and early childhood education research. In S. A. Kessler & B. B. Swadener (Eds.), *Reconceptualizing the early childhood curriculum: Beginning the dialogue* (pp. 3–20). Teachers College Press.

Bonello, C. (2018). *Boys and early literacy learning in three Maltese state schools* (PhD thesis). University of Sheffield.

Bonello, C. (2019). A paradigm paralysis? Boys and early literacy learning in three Maltese state schools. *Malta Review of Educational Research, 13*(1), 79–107.

Bonello, C. (2021). Democracy or legacy? Boys' views on early literacy in three Maltese state schools. *Journal of Early Childhood Research*. https://doi.org/10.1177/1476718X211051330.

Bonello, C., Deguara, J., Farrugia, R., Gatt, S., Tania, M., Milton, J., Said, L., & Spiteri, J. (2021). *Exploring the influence of COVID-19 on initial teacher education in Malta: Student participation in higher education*. Paper presented at the 7th International Conference on Higher Education Advances (HEAd'21). http://doi.org/10.4995/HEAd21.2021.12794

Braun, V., & Clarke, V. (2006). Using thematic analysis in psychology. *Qualitative Research in Psychology, 3*(2), 77–101.

Brooker, L. (2001). Interviewing children. In G. MacNaughton, S. Rolfe, & I. Siraj-Blatchford (Eds.), *Doing early childhood research: International perspectives on theory and practice* (pp. 162–167). Open University Press.

Bryman, A. (2016). *Social research methods* (5th ed.). Oxford University Press.

Caldwell, J. C., Harrison, G. E., & Quiggin, P. (1980). The demography of microstates. *World Development, 8,* 953–968.

Calleja, J. (1994). The evolution of education in Malta: A philosophy in the making. In *Revue du monde Musulman et da la la Méditerranée, n°71, 1994. le carrefour Maltais* (pp. 185–197). DOI : https://doi.org/10.3406/remmm.1994.1643

Cannella, G. S. (1997). *Deconstructing early childhood education: Social justice and revolution.* Peter Lang.

Chomsky, N. (2016). *Who rules the world?* Hamish Hamilton (Penguin Books).

Cohen, L., Manion, L., & Morrison, K. (2007). *Research methods in education* (6th ed.). Routledge.

Creswell, J. W., & Plano Clark, V. L. (2011). *Designing and conducting mixed methods research* (2nd ed.). SAGE.

Cutajar, M. (2007). Educational reform in the Maltese islands. *Journal of Maltese Education Research, 5*(1), 3–21.

Directorate for Quality and Standards in Education [DQSE]. (2009). *National policy and strategy for the attainment of core competences in primary education.* Ministry for Education, Culture, Youth and Sport. https://education.gov.mt/en/resources/Documents/Policy%20Documents/Attai%20Core_Competencies.pdf

Directorate for Quality and Standards in Education [DQSE]. (2015). *Learning outcomes framework [LOF].* Ministry for Education, Culture, Youth and Sport.

Ehri, L. C. (1995). Phases of development in learning to read words by sight. *Journal of Research in Reading, 18*(2), 116–125.

European Commission. (2017). *Future of Europe: Towards a European education area by 2025.* http://europa.eu/rapid/press-release_IP-17-4521_en.htm

Eurostat. (2020). *Archive: Europe 2020 indicators – Malta.* https://ec.europa.eu/eurostat/statistics-explained/index.php?title=Archive:Europe_2020_indicators_-_Malta&oldid=345786

Freire, P. (1970). *Pedagogy of the oppressed.* New York: Seabury Press.

Gee, J. P. (1991). *Social linguistics: Ideology in discourses.* Falmer Press.

Gold, R. M. (1958). Roles in sociological field observations. *Social Forces,* 217–23.

Gupta, A. (2013). *Early childhood education, postcolonial theory, teaching practices and policies in India: Balancing Vygotsky and the Veda* (2nd ed.). Palgrave Macmillan.

Hart, R. A. (1997). *Children's participation: The theory and practice of involving young citizens in community development and environmental care.* London: UNICEF; Earthscan.

Harvey, J. (1999). *Civilized oppression.* New York and Oxford: Rowman and Littlefield Publishers.

Hunkin, E. (2018). Whose quality? The (mis)uses of quality reform in early childhood and education policy. *Journal of Education Policy, 33*(4), 443–456. https://doi.org/10.1080/02680939.2017.1352032.

International Reading Association. (n.d.). Honouring children's rights to excellent reading instruction. *reading rockets.org.* www.readingrockets.org/article/honoring-childrens-rights-excellent-reading-instruction-0

Kano, Y. (2006). *Curriculum as cultural practice.* University of Toronto Press Incorporated.

Kaomea, J. (2003). Reading erasures and making the familiar strange: Defamiliarizing methods for research in formerly colonized and historically oppressed communities. *Educational Researcher, 32*(2), 14–25.

Keenan, P. J. (1879). *Report upon the Educational System of Malta.* Dublin: Alexander Thom.

Laevers, F. (1994). *Defining and assessing quality in early childhood education.* Leuven University Press.

Larson, J., & Marsh, J. (2015). *Making literacy real: Theories and practices for learning and teaching* (2nd ed.). SAGE.

Laurenza, V. (1939). *Cio' che l'istruzione in Malta deve alla chiesa.* Empire Press.

Loomba, A. (1998). *Colonialism/postcolonialism.* Routledge.

Lubeck, S. (1985). *Sandbox society: Early education in black and white America.* Falmer Press.

Macedo, D. (1999). Decolonizing indigenous knowledge. In L. Semali & J. L. Kincheloe (Eds.), *What is indigenous knowledge: Voices from the academy* (pp. xi–xvi). Falmer Press.

MacNaughton, G. (2000). *Rethinking gender in early childhood education.* Allen & Ulwin.

Maltatoday. (2012). *To know us is to know the English.* www.maltatoday.com.mt/arts/books/23105/to-know-us-is-to-know-the-english-20121203#.YXKjWS2w2Rt

McGregor, H. E., & Marker, M. (2018). Reciprocity in indigenous educational research: Beyond compensation, towards decolonizing. *Anthropology & Education Quarterly, 49*(3), 318–328. https://doi.org/10.1111/aeq.12249.

Mifsud, C., Milton, J., Brooks, G., & Hutchison, D. (2000). *Literacy in Malta: The 1999 national survey of the attainment of year 2 pupils.* University of Malta.

Mignolo, W. D. (2011). Geopolitics of sensing and knowing: On (de)coloniality, border thinking and epistemic disobedience. *Postcolonial Studies, 14*(3), 273–283.

Millard, E. (1997). Differently literate: Gender identity and the construction of the developing reader. *Gender and Education, 9*(1), 31–48.

Ministry for Education and Employment (MEDE). (1999). *National minimum curriculum.* Salesian Press.

Ministry for Education and Employment (MEDE). (2006). *Early childhood education and care: A national policy.* Author.

Ministry for Education and Employment, (MEDE). (2012). *A national curriculum framework for all.* Salesian Press. https://curriculum.gov.mt/en/Resources/The-NCF/Documents/NCF.pdf

Ministry for Education and Employment (MEDE). (2015). *Learning outcomes framework: About the learning outcomes framework.* www.schools.learningoutcomes.edu.mt. www.schoolslearningoutcomes.edu.mt/en/pages/about-the-framework

Ministry for Education and Employment (MEDE). (2024). *Framework for the education strategy for Malta 2014–2024: Sustaining foundations, creating alternatives, increasing employability.* Ministry for Education and Employment. https://education.gov.mt/en/resources/Documents/Policy%20Documents%202014/BOOKLET%20ESM%202014-2024%20ENG%2019-02.pdf

Ministry for the Family, Children's Rights and Social Solidarity. (2017). *National Children's Policy.* https://cdn-others.timesofmalta.com/67cacf015f1719f5fee468a35d3306e4fbd85f1c.pdf

Monbiot, G. (2017). *Out of the wreckage: A new politics for an age of crisis.* Verso.

Nkrumah, K. (1965). *Neo-colonialism: The last stage of imperialism.* Thomas Nelson & Sons Ltd.

Nutbrown, C. (1996). *Respectful educators, capable learners: Children's rights and early education.* Paul Chapman.

Nxumalo, F. & Adair, J. K. (2018). Social justice and equity in early childhood education. In C. P. Brown, M. McMullen, & N. File (Eds.), *Handbook of early childhood care and education.* Hoboken: Wiley Blackwell.

Organisation for Economic Co-operation and Development (OECD). (2018). *Starting strong: Early childhood education and care.* Author.

Pacini-Ketchabaw, V., & Taylor, A. (2015). *Unsettling the colonial places and spaces of early childhood education* (1st ed.). Routledge. https://doi.org/10.4324/9781315771342

Palmer, S. (2016). *Upstart: The case for raising the school starting age and providing what the under-sevens really need.* Floris Books.

Papen, U. (2005). Literacy and development: What works for whom? Or, how relevant is the social practices view of literacy for literacy education in developing countries? *International Journal of Educational Development, 25*(1), 5–17. https://doi.org/10.1016/j.ijedudev.2004.05.001

Pence, A. (2011). Early childhood care and development research in Africa: Historical, conceptual, and structural challenges. *Child Development Perspective, 5*(2), 112–118. https://doi.org/10.1111/j.1750-8606.2011.00165.x

Pullicino, P. (1850). *Rapporto sulla educazione primaria nelle isole di Malta e Gozo. Malta.* Available at NAM, General Miscellaneous Reports, Report No. 35.

Robert-Holmes, G. (2005). *Doing your early years research project: A step by step guide.* SAGE.

Roberts, P. (1995). Defining literacy: Paradise, nightmare or red herring? *British Journal of Educational Studies, 43*(4), 412–432.

Rogers, M., Dovigo, F., & Doan, L. (2020). Educator identity in a neoliberal context: Recognising and supporting early childhood education and care education. *European Early Childhood Education Research Journal, 28*(6), 806–822.

Rugut, E. J., & Osman, A. A. (2013). Reflection on Paulo Freire and classroom relevance. *American International Journal of Social Science, 2*(2), 23–28.

Said, E. W. (2003). *Orientalism.* Penguin Classics.

Sartre, J. P. (2005). *Colonialism and neocolonialism* (1st ed.). Taylor and Francis.

Seremani, T. W., & Clegg, S. (2015). Postcolonialism, organization, and management theory the role of "epistemological third spaces". *Journal of Management Inquiry, 25,* 171–183. https://doi.org/10.1177/1056492615589973.

Shaw, C., Braidy, L., & Davey, C. (2011). *Guidelines for research with children and young people.* NCB Research Centre.

Sims, M. (2017). Neoliberalism and early childhood. *Cogent Education, 4,* 1–10. https://doi.org/10.1080/2331186.2017.1365411.

Smith, A. B. (2017). Children's rights and early childhood education. In L. Miller, C. Cameron, C. Dalli, & N. Barbour (Eds.), *The Sage handbook of early childhood policy* (pp. 452–464). SAGE.

Sollars, V. (2018). Shaping early childhood education services in Malta: Historical events, current affairs, future challenges. *Early Years,* 1–14. https://doi.org/10.1080/09575146.2018.1512561

Street, B. V. (1984). *Literacy in theory and practice.* Cambridge University Press.
Street, B. V. (2003). What's "new" in new literacy studies? Critical approaches to literacy in theory and practice. *Current Issues in Comparative Education, 5*(2), 77–91.
Sultana, G. R. (1997). *Inside/outside schools* (new edition). P.E.G. Ltd.
The Malta Independent. (2018). *Why do men account for 88% of suicides in Malta?* www.independent.com.mt/articles/2018-02-11/local-news/Why-do-men-account-for-88-of-suicides-in-Malta-6736184698
The Open University. (n.d.). *Language and literacy in a changing world.* www.open.edu/openlearncreate/mod/oucontent/view.php?id=15196&section=2.2.1
Times of Malta. (2018). 150 years of prayer and service in aid of people in need. *The Times of Malta.* https://timesofmalta.com/articles/view/150-years-of-prayer-and-service-in-aid-of-people-in-need.695715
Times of Malta. (2020). *Reading, science, maths: Malta's education system ranks poorly.* https://timesofmalta.com/articles/view/education-system-in-the-dock-as-students-score-low-in-major-survey.774464
Times of Malta. (2021). Educational reforms in Malta in the late 1830s. *Times of Malta.* https://timesofmalta.com/articles/view/educational-reforms-in-malta-in-the-late-1830s.801054
Tobin, J. (2011). Understanding a human rights based approach to matters involving children: Conceptual foundations and strategic consdierations. In A. Invernizzi & J. Williams (Eds.), *The human rights of children: From vision to implementation* (pp. 61–98). Farnham: Ashgate.
United Nations. (1989). *Convention on the rights of the child.* https://www2.ohchr.org/english/bodies/crc/docs/AdvanceVersions/GeneralComment7Rev1.pdf
Viruru, R. (2005). The impact of postcolonial theory on early childhood education. *Journal of Education, 35,* 7–30.
Weaver-Hightower, M. (2003). The "boy turn" in research on gender and education. *Review of Educational Research, 73*(4), 471–498.
Wolstein, A. (2017). *Decolonizing literacy instruction.* https://din.today/news/decolonizing-literacy-education/.
Woodhead, M., & Moss, P. (2007). *Early childhood and primary education: Transitions in the lives of young children* (No. 2). Open University.
Zammit Ciantar, J. (Ed.). (1993). *Education in Malta (a handbook).* Salesian Press.
Zammit Mangion, J. (1992). *Education in Malta.* MANSPRINT.

2 'Rough' or 'prim and proper'? Unpacking popular explanations for the gender gap in literacy attainment in a Maltese early years context

Chapter Overview

This chapter evaluates how contemporary popular explanations for the gender gap in literacy attainment feature in the discourses of several stakeholders in a Maltese context. Triangulated quantitative and qualitative data from an online questionnaire, classroom observations, individual interviews and focus groups provide a snapshot into the shades of gender and early literacy amongst educators, heads of school, heads of department (literacy) and parents of boys in Maltese state schools. Findings indicate that the majority of discourses were grounded in essentialist mindsets and traditional gender stereotypes in early literacy learning, favouring girls. The chapter unveils a hidden duality in power relations within schooled early literacy, perpetuating postcolonial legacies that may negatively impact the lifelong literate identities of young children – particularly boys. The key argument revolves around a need for critical consciousness and critical activism for social justice in gender and early literacy learning. It is argued that the advocacy potential of children's rights and postcolonial theory may assist in the creation of new spaces to deconstruct and reconstruct new ways of thinking, grounded in Freire's philosophy of education for liberation. Implications are discussed to visualise new possibilities and guide several stakeholders in education who seek to decolonise – through collective action – overlooked accepted truths and a legacy of hierarchical gender binarism in early literacy learning. It attempts to evoke interest in the often overlooked issue of gender in ECEC and ECEC curricula in the majority of countries (Connolly, 2004; Yelland, 1998).

DOI: 10.4324/9781003125525-2

Teaching young children provided me with several eyewitness accounts to consider how some stakeholders viewed young boys' literacy, and what factors may be influencing the shaping of the boys' identities and attitudes towards literacy learning. Against this background, I felt a pressing need to explore gendered discourse[1] on literacy learning in the shadows of popular explanations for the gender gap in literacy attainment within a Maltese ECEC context. Children's gender development in the early years is an important period (Perry et al., 2019). It is a fitting period of time for reducing the gender gaps in different areas of learning (Master et al., 2017). Thus, it is important to examine any gendered discourse that plays a key role in influencing young children's literate identities across cultures and contexts. Through a gender-responsive[2] (United Nations Development Programme, 2015) effort, I draw on the findings of my doctoral work to re-examine discovered gender bias and power dynamics in gender roles from a children's rights and postcolonial perspective. This re-examination process is an attempt to move towards more gender inclusiveness in schooled early literacy – an often-unnoticed area of knowledge.

Explanations for the gender gap in literacy attainment and its influence on boys and early literacy

As stated in the previous chapter, the gender gap in literacy attainment persists, with Malta having one of the widest gender gaps in literacy attainment (favouring girls) (OECD, 2018). Research shows that some girls underachieve, too, whilst others exceed their high targets with relative ease. Nevertheless, national and international literacy tests highlight the literacy difficulties of individual children, the majority of whom are boys. Such evidence and popular stereotypes and ingrained perceptions about boys and literacy create binary gender constructs and disguise the social, cultural and political elements influencing literacy practices and the shaping of identities being negotiated in various sites, including those outside of school (Charles, 2007). To this end, it is important to understand the links between individual accounts and the wider discourses on boys and literacy at the national and global level (Saukko, 2003). Explanations for this popular gender gap are presented in literature through varied theoretical positions to inform classroom literacy practice. For example, in a study on boys and literacy, Alloway et al. (2002) suggested that the issue of gender literacy differences can be explained in terms of neuroscientific studies, availability of role models in schools, sociocultural and socioeconomic circumstances and educational experiences (see Figure 2.1). This framework will be used in this chapter to present a summary of the views of several stakeholders on boys and early literacy learning with a Maltese state school scenario.

Such explanations for the gender gap in literacy achievement are underpinned by essentialist (the perspective that there are pre-conceived

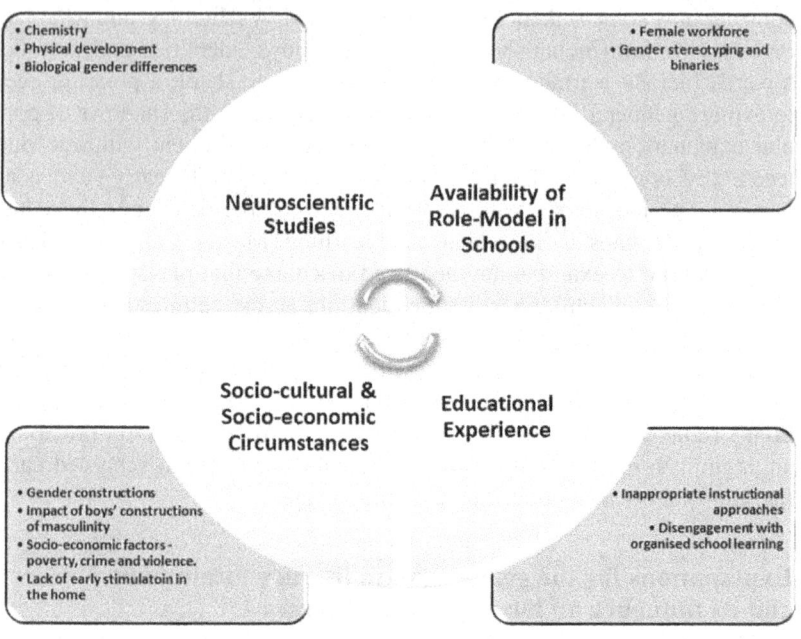

Figure 2.1 Explanations for the gender difference in literacy (Alloway et al., 2002)

biological and physiological differences between boys and girls), and anti-essentialist mindsets (the view that behaviours displayed by girls and boys are a production of diverse social and cultural contexts). Popular essentialist explanations led to moral panic and global attempts to eradicate the gender gap in literacy through approaches that include male role models, single-sex classes, boys' interests and boy-friendly approaches to literacy instruction (Martino, 2008). In view of the above, one of my research questions in my doctoral research study was the following:

> What is the relationship between the rhetoric on boys' underachievement (in media and educational research) and Maltese state school teachers' beliefs in, and practices of, boys and literacy in the early primary years?

The findings emerging as a response to this question, triggered more connected questions following the completion of my study:

• Do the stakeholders' dominant socially constructed discourses on boys and early literacy have any connections with Malta's colonial past?

- How is this gendered discourse featured when filtered through the philosophy underpinning the UNCRC?

- How can a child's rights lens and postcolonial theory contribute to reconceptualising the unmasked gendered discourse, and rethink boys' underachievement in literacy within a Maltese early years context?

This chapter is an attempt to investigate further by seeking to answer these follow-up questions through a re-examination of the doctoral findings that relate to social constructions on boys and literacy learning from the dual lens of children's rights and postcolonial theory.

Given the contested nature of the argument in this chapter, I would like to point out that the decision to focus on boys, literacy and gendered discourse originates from the curiosity to challenge and face the hegemonic local and global discourse on boys' underachievement in literacy performance. It is an attempt to search for knowledge to unravel the roots of dominant gendered discourses in schooled early literacy, and identify possible ways forward through deep experiential insights from several stakeholders in a postcolonial context.

Social constructions of gender, stereotyping and dominant discourse in the early years

In this book, gender is perceived as a social construct whereby the social context affects who you are, your identity and the way you think and act (Fine, 2010). Young children experience the challenge to act as 'typical' girls and boys due to the dominant discourses related to masculinity and femininity within their cultures. Gender stereotyping leads to set gender differences starting from the age of two and-a-half years (Mulvey & Killen, 2015). Parents, educators, peers and the media usually promulgate stereotypical concepts of gender (Heyman & Legare, 2004). The quality of the interactions, stereotypical discriminatory comments, biased educators' evaluation of performance and the tonality used in classrooms, which is often linked to gender-based differences, are also perceived as an influential factor in the learning process (Matějů & Smith, 2015; Younger et al., 1999). Research shows that educators' dominant masculine discourse, and social constructs of misbehaving boys that show less interest in education, may influence boys' performance in literacy (Warson-Williams & Riddell, 2011). Such biased views and binary constructions of gender have been identified in educators' classroom discourse where, conversely, girls are seen as more compliant to schooling (Younger & Cobbett, 2014). It is important to question how and why gender differences in literate identities arise through an examination of adult discourse and adult-child classroom talk constructed in diverse ECEC contexts.

Gender, literacy, power, children's rights and postcolonial theory

Viruru's work (Cannella & Viruru, 2004; Viruru, 2001) has revealed how ECEC, on a global level, has been impacted by dominant Western discourses in relation to young children. Viruru (2005, p. 7) captures the chemistry between ECEC, power relations and postcolonial theory as follows:

> a key concept in postcolonial theory, an unmasking of the will to power, that essentializes diverse ways of viewing and living in the world, is related to the field of early childhood education.

As a postcolonial scholar, Viruru's work made me ask: Whose power is dominant when it comes to gender discourse and early literacy learning within postcolonial ECEC contexts, like Malta, and how is this affecting young boys and girls? Research indicates that early childhood pedagogies influence gendered power relations within schools and the gendering of boys' and girls' literate identities (MacNaughton, 2000). In the same way, inequitable power relations at home may also influence boys' and girls' negotiations of their literate identities. According to Freire (1985), gaining an understanding of the world must take precedence to learning to read and write. A critical pedagogy permeates educators to help their learners gain a deeper insight into contemporary injustices reproduced from social power relations, and structures created in past times. In tandem with Article 2 in the UNCRC, arguments in research and policy highlight global concerns related to fairness in early childhood pedagogic practice (Langford, 2010; Dahlberg et al., 2007):

> All children have all these rights, no matter who they are, where they live, what language they speak, what their religion is, what they think, what they look like, if they are a boy or girl, if they have a disability, if they are rich or poor, and no matter who their parents or families are or what their parents or families believe or do. No child should be treated unfairly for any reason.
>
> (United Nations, 1989)

Findings from the broader doctoral work, will be re-examined through the values underpinning the statement in Article 2 of the UNCRC to unveil the roots of dominant powers in gender and schooled early literacy in Maltese state schools. The advocacy potential of the UNCRC is also taken into account. In this chapter, I argue that there is the need to rethink how boys are being conceptualised as literacy learners from their earliest years to challenge a reinforced legacy of hierarchical gender binarism within schooled literacy learning in Malta – like other countries, an ex-colony that signed the UNCRC over thirty years ago but is still grappling with the challenge to fulfil its realisation in ECEC practice.

Popular explanations for the gender gap in literacy attainment intersect the discourse on schooled early literacy in a postcolonial Maltese state school scenario

This chapter will draw on data collected through an online questionnaire, interviews and focus groups with several stakeholders in 2017 as part of my doctoral project (see Chapter 1 for an elaborated version of the methodology used for this study). For the purposes of this chapter, a triangulation of the largely qualitative and quantitative findings from the three tools will be presented below, and subsequently re-examined through a child's rights and postcolonial lens. The presented data outlines the stakeholders' discourse in view of the popular explanations for the gender gap in literacy attainment within a Maltese state school scenario. I would like to point out that the purpose of this chapter is not to critique the views of stakeholders in Malta on how they position themselves within the boys and literacy worldwide agenda. Instead, it aims to take these local statements as a representation of the global discourses available in the social media and literature and see what can be learned from the ways in which postcolonial stakeholders positioned their conceptualisations of boys as literacy learners in a Maltese ECEC context.

Biological/developmental and role model explanations for the gender gap in literacy achievement within a postcolonial Maltese state school scenario

The first statement in the questionnaire presented a neuroscientific claim. Figure 2.2 indicates that 43% (83 out of 192 teachers) preferred to remain neutral, while 28% (54 out of 192 teachers) believed that the difference between girls' and boys' brain development influenced boys' early literacy learning. The remaining 18% (34 out of 192 teachers) opposed.

This suggests that a higher percentage of early primary teachers tended to view the innate biological differences between the sexes as a dominant factor that influences boys' literacy attainment. Findings from the face-to-face interviews also revealed a marginalised perspective grounded in boys' and

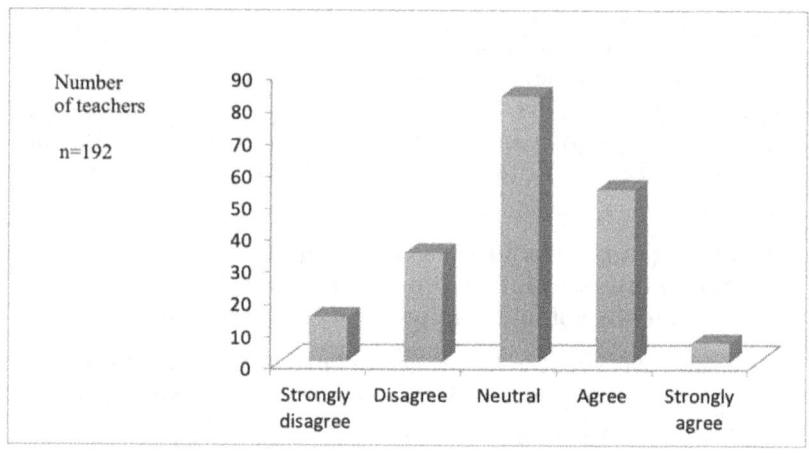

Figure 2.2 Online questionnaire statement one: The difference between boys' and girls' brain development account for boys' early literacy learning

girls' biological/developmental aspects as one of the reasons that might lead to future gender gaps in literacy attainment:

> I think that boys in the early years take longer to develop so that might be another factor. Boys' development in early years is slower than that of girls.
>
> Mr Mario, Head of School, Sawrella School

Similarly, most parents agreed with the principle that children are born with innate characteristics, natural personalities and intellectual and moral qualities that impact their future performance in literacy attainment. Parallel claims are evident in previously published scholarly work (Gurian, 2001; Skolverket, 2006). Likewise, Figure 2.3 reveals that there were more educators in favour of having more adult men involved with boys' literacy, as 36.8% agreed (71 out of 193 teachers) and 30.1% (58 out of 193 teachers) disagreed.

Accordingly, during the interviews and focus groups, several stakeholders assumed a strong status regarding the absence of male educators in schools and home, and noted how this had an adverse effect on the boys' engagement and performance in reading and writing:

> Yes, I believe it would. We don't have it though. I believe that we would see a difference in the students' progress if we had more males in the education system.
>
> Ms Charlene, Head of Department, literacy, Sawrella School

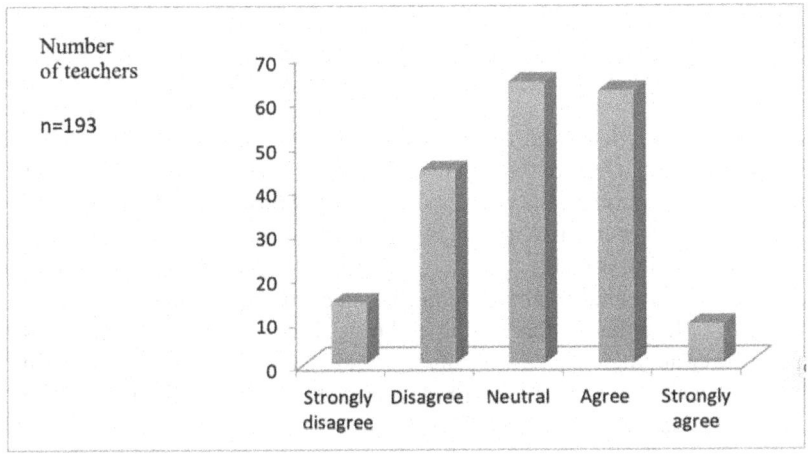

Figure 2.3 Online questionnaire statement five: If more adult men were involved with teaching/volunteering to role model and support boys in reading and writing activities, boys' literacy learning would improve

Conversely, some professionals suggested that boys might prefer female educators, 'the mother figure', and that in a mixed-gender school system male educators might be disengaging girls. The majority of the data shows that stakeholders from the three state schools were more likely to relate their provided explanations for boys' underachievement to the need for boys to be exposed to male role models to engage them more and improve their early literacy learning. Alloway et al. (2002) claimed that if schools draw upon influential role-model theories to understand boys' underachievement they would never be able to adopt a broader view that would allow for the improvement of literacy teaching and learning. There is no specific research claiming that male educators improve learners' academic achievement (Brownhill, 2016; Martino, 2008) and other scholars argued that sex differences do not determine educators' competence, and thus it is not the solution to eradicate illiteracy for boys (Francis, 2008; Rowe, 2001).

The fallacy of connecting constructions of boys' underachievement and literacy performance with development through the dual lens of children's rights and postcolonial theory

Findings strongly indicate that universal biological/developmental explanations were largely common amongst professionals working in the early primary sector and parents in Maltese state schools. These explanations, grounded in a positivist child development worldview, were believed to be a crucial factor in determining boys' and girls' performance in literacy. Child development emanating from positivist research is a means of dominating one group over another (Cannella, 1997). Indeed, boys seem to be viewed as a group that does not progress at the same pace as girls in literacy due to their development, and this engenders a dialogue that is culturally and socially unjust. The homogeneous claim that 'girls are quicker to learn' was common amongst the respondents. From a postcolonial lens and with several reconceptualist scholars (Bloch, 1992; Lubeck, 1994), I argue that developmental psychology and Euro-Western mainstream ideologies, based on the truth-oriented hypothesis that humans can be judged, may be supporting the legacies of dominating enduring dichotomies that privilege one group over another. As Viruru (2005, p. 21) claims: 'The idea that in some cultures, equating childhood with development is culturally inappropriate, is not considered'.

One example is the universalist discourse underpinning the Developmentally Appropriate Practice (DAP) guidelines issued by the National Association for the Education of Young Children (NAEYC) in the United States. These dominating and oppressing guidelines narrow possibilities for children, families and ECEC at a global level (Lubeck, 1985; Shallwani, 2010). To this end, stakeholders in education need to be mindful of the contemporary diverse shapes and forms of oppression and control that can be traced in the historical backdrops of their context. As evident in this chapter, dominant gendered discourse on early literacy within a Maltese postcolonial context – a reproduction of imperialism (Shallwani, 2010) – may be limiting the literate lives of some boys.

Findings suggest that the emerging neoliberal power relations underpinning the moral panic on boys and literacy, and the popular rhetoric on biological/developmental explanations filtered into the lives of adults and children in a postcolonial Maltese ECEC context, increase the risk of preserving more colonial truths. As Viruru (2005, p. 16) claims, 'dominant ideologies of how children grow and develop have become another of colonialism's truths that permit no questioning, and that are imposed unhesitatingly upon people around the world for their own good'.

If essentialist worldviews (i.e., all boys or boys only) are adopted as acceptable explanations to educators and other professionals in our education system, these may give rise to implications on the existing and future literacy learning of young boys (Alloway et al., 2002; Fine, 2010; Hempel-Jorgensen et al., 2017; Langford, 2010), as well as girls.

Within a child's rights philosophy, the standardised descriptions on the groups of boys and girls, based on developmental assumptions, result in discrimination within early literacy practice (Article 2, United Nations, 1989) in a postcolonial context. I argue that the developing argument grounded in postcolonial theory and the potentiality of Article 2 in the UNCRC may serve as the driving force needed for more nuanced understandings, inquiry and change in the way boys are presently being conceptualised within the field of early literacy learning in a Maltese context.

Sociocultural, socioeconomic and the educational experience as explanations to boys' underachievement and literacy achievement within a postcolonial Maltese state school scenario

While biology and role model theories were perceived by a significant number of stakeholders to be crucial in determining boys' and girls' future literacy performance, some others believed that educational, sociocultural, and socioeconomic explanations were influential in young boys' literacy learning. Figure 2.4 shows that 49.3% (95 out of 193 respondents) concur with research indicating that girls fare better than boys in reading and writing (Dent, 2017; MEDE, 2013; Mifsud, 2000).

Open-ended comments in the online questionnaire indicated evidence of similar claims on boys and their educational experience in early literacy learning in Matlese state schools:

> I find that boys may have less concentration and so they will need more help from complementary (literacy) teachers.
>
> Teacher, respondent to online questionnaire

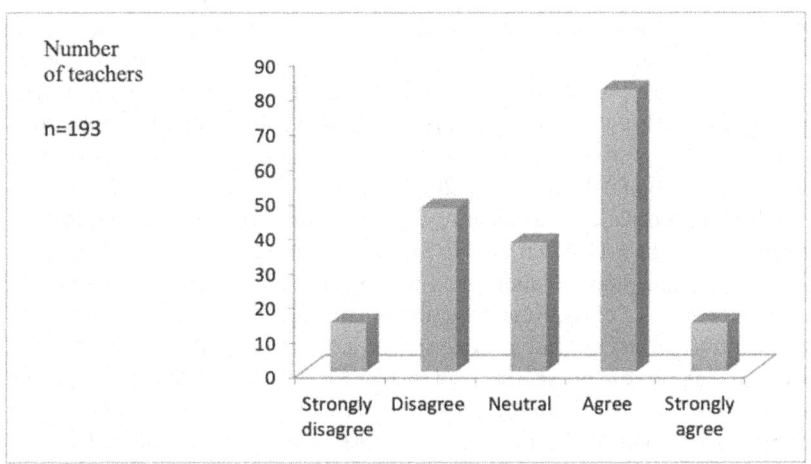

Figure 2.4 Online questionnaire statement six: Some boys have more difficulty with reading and writing than girls do

Some other teacher respondents to the online questionnaire promoted 'boy-friendly' strategies. For example, one teacher commented that the 'majority of boys tend to be more technical and that educators should focus on these topics to get the boys on board in a literacy programme'. Pennycook (2011) points out that if teachers position themselves within discourses that promote boy-friendly strategies to minimise the statistical gender gap, 'a neoliberal agenda of recuperative masculinity is reinstated in the classroom, and gender justice is no longer served' (p. 11). Other stakeholders based their explanations for boys' underachievement in literacy performance on inappropriate instructional approaches in Maltese schools:

> I remember I had a group of boys in a complementary (literacy) session and one of them told me 'It is quite boring here' – he was talking about his classroom teaching and his homework. I used to do guided reading with them, higher order thinking skills, etc. he enjoyed that.
>
> Ms Joanne, Head of Department, literacy, Rużetta School

Findings show that professionals rather than parents raised the issue around present pedagogies in Maltese state schools, and the concern that such a formal one-size-fits-all system is not enabling boys to reach their full potential. Parents have also reported comments like 'girls in our school system fit in a better way'. The three heads of department (literacy) interviewed specifically agreed that sound early years' pedagogy is crucial in determining progress in boys' literacy learning, and that the current formal system is not allowing young children, particularly boys, to flourish when it comes to reading and writing practices. It was also observed in these comments that some professionals tended to refer to boys and also girls as a homogeneous group of learners. As previous research and literature pointed out, this might have implications in the way the diverse needs of different boys and different girls, across diverse cultures and contexts, are perceived in schooled literacy learning (Alloway et al., 2002; Cigman, 2014).

Classroom practice is a space where social messages may be reinforced. In the early years, children absorb messages through classroom discourse. These messages may be underlined by power and privilege when it comes to gender, race or class. According to Hyland (2010) 'The consequences of these messages are enormous not only for individual children, but also for a society that strives for equality and justice for all' (p. 82). Dominant power relations are evident in the following excerpt from a recorded observation conducted in one of the three Year 1 classrooms that participated in this study:

Table 2.1 Excerpt from a recorded classroom observation during a Maltese lesson in one state school – Year 1 classroom (five- to six-year-olds)

Awwista School: Maltese grammar lesson

Ms Connie told the children that she wanted to see how neatly they could write by copying the eight sentences she was writing in different colours on the whiteboard. The date, title of the lesson and the eight sentences were prepared on the interactive whiteboard for the children to copy. In the meantime, the four boys observed played with their pencils or talked to their peers. The classroom assistant distributed the narrow-lined copybooks and sat down between Matthew and Paul to help them. Ms Connie explained that they were going to work out the grammar exercise orally together and then they had to work them out independently. Isaac asked: 'Do we have P.E. lesson today'? (Physical education session outdoors with another teacher). The teacher refused to answer as he asked the same question several times during that day. During the oral explanation, Paul started to chew on his pencil and the other three boys seemed absent. Ms Connie had to draw the attention of some of the boys observed during her explanation to have them sit down and listen carefully. After the explanation they were told to start off using their pencil and copybooks. Ms Connie took their mathematics workbook and sat at her desk correcting, while all the children started their writing task independently. Matthew took out his bottle to drink. Tim got out of his place and walked around the classroom chewing his pencil. He was told to go back to his place and continue his work. After some time, Ms Connie went round the classroom to check on their work, and pointed out that the boys' work was messier and that they were not writing in the narrow line. Girls were praised for their neat writing. Paul started to scribble on his copybook instead of copying the sentences. He was told to rub off everything. Tim seemed confused and rubbed off everything too. Ms Connie asked why he rubbed it off. Tim just looked at her. The teacher informed the children that they are working on sentences now and that the work is getting harder. The children were also told that if they will be good, they would be given permission to use the play dough after the lesson. The whole group was thrilled and yelled: 'Yeah'! The children who were ready before their peers were told to work on a worksheet or do some colouring-in. The lesson ended after 90 minutes.

In this excerpt (see Table 2.1), we see evidence of how the concerned boys were being exposed to a top-down literacy curriculum eliminating the possibility that their experiential knowledge is taken into account. Through a postcolonial lens, it can be argued that the witnessed gender power relations in early literacy pedagogy reproduces a case of colonisation within early years classrooms. Pedagogy may influence some young boys' gender and literate identities, as well as gender power relations in early literacy learning (MacNaughton, 2000). Similar findings emerged from the other two Year 1 classrooms situated in another two Maltese state schools. During similar passive classroom literacy tasks, boys were often told off. Girls were praised for their sitting tolerance, for being quicker in their reading and writing tasks and for writing neater. Several scholars affirmed that boys are being harmed by schools that are feminised (Biddulph, 1997; Brownhill, 2016; Pollack, 1998), and that this might be promoting some stereotypical feminine ways that might influence boys' literate identities and their reading and writing performance (Evans & Davies, 2000; Millard, 1997; Zambo & Brozo, 2009).

Furthermore, such pupil labelling in relation to what constitutes an 'ideal pupil' (Becker, 1952) for teachers within dominant classroom pedagogies, may lead to blaming if the pupils concerned do not fit classroom standards (Hempel-Jorgensen, 2009). Brooker (2005) suggested that 'rethinking the characteristics we value in children would require us to rethink the entrenched cultural bias shown in our provision of learning' (p. 127). Thus, it is critical for teachers to examine and retain consciousness of the impact such discourses have on the way the ideal pupil is constructed within classrooms characterised by extreme hierarchical positioning (Hempel-Jorgensen, 2015). Perhaps it is time to unsettle ourselves from comfortable hegemonic or change-resistant discourses, and not simply continue to pay lip service to what is fair and just. Instead, should we not move to a position where we try to provide a literate educational journey that is receptive and inclusive in its everyday practices?

From Freire's (1970) viewpoint, the presented findings reveal a situation where, through talk, young boys are positioned as the oppressed in early literacy education. If this unjust situation is overlooked, it may increase the risk of having boys who may grow into feeling fine with this lived social oppression. They would then have already internalised the consciousness of the oppressor. In time, there is no harm for them in being a male who is not neat when writing or disinterested in reading. As McLaren (2002) points out: 'the powerful win the consent of those who are oppressed, with the oppressed unknowingly participating in their own oppression' (p. 67). Therefore, it can be argued that some boys may internalise the assumption that reading and writing is more fitting for girls. Findings from the online questionnaire in this study show that 9.3% (18 out of 193) early primary educators indicated that some young boys already think so. Hyland (2010, p. 82) stresses that:

> it is essential that early childhood educators continue to develop practices and pedagogies that address the educational injustices that plague children from historically marginalized groups and that teachers examine the value-laden messages in everyday practices in order to create more just learning environments.

All children have the right to be themselves without ending up in an inferior position in early literacy education influenced by postcolonial mental models (Article 2, United Nations, 1989). Laevers and Verboven (2000) point out that unconscious attitudes and behaviours of educators and parents, the distribution of gender roles in households and the influence of today's media all support gender inequality. It is interesting to note that findings from their study indicate that teachers discriminate less between girls and boys when implementing an experiential approach to education compared to a more traditional approach. Early childhood educators need to see themselves as decolonising educators to free early literacy learning from gender and other discriminations in postcolonial contexts. This may be taken-for-granted if they ground their claims in other explanations for the gender gap in literacy. For example, a number of teachers complied with the argument that the solution to keeping up with the school's literacy requirements and perform well at early primary level is highly dependent on the families' commitment at home.

Professionals from Maltese state schools also spoke about financial stability and the helplessness of families with a low socioeconomic status to prepare their children for the literacy demands of schooling in early primary. This notion corresponded to local research where it was evident that Maltese children from low socioeconomic backgrounds struggled in their literacy attainment at school (Mifsud et al., 2004). Whilst some scholars believe that pedagogical and socioeconomic factors are key to the improvement of boys' literacy learning, others suggest that a change in the social and cultural experiences of the child might narrow the gap (Smyth, 2007; Sommers, 2000). Some stakeholders theorised that social constructions of femininity and masculinity affected boys' learning, engagement or attitudes towards literacy:

> Boys tend to be more nonchalant about school than girls and maybe that is how they view schooling even from a tender age as theirs . . . boys tend to have a 'rougher' approach towards school while girls should always be prim and proper.
>
> Teacher, respondent to online questionnaire

Such claims show constructed marginalised views on masculinity within Maltese schooled early literacy learning, and it is likely that within these statements boys were being stereotypically positioned as a homogeneous group that is disengaged from academics. In view of this argument, Claxton (2008) pointed out the hazardous mistake educators make when they confuse disengagement with the learners' performance and abilities.

Unwished-for, male-oriented behaviour in early literacy tasks, or 'undesirable practices' as termed by Alloway et al. (2002, p. 98), were also seen as factors that influenced boys' literacy performance in a Maltese context:

> I had boys who performed quite well in early literacy tasks. However, on the whole girls perform better than boys. The attention of girls is much better, they want everything done neatly, in order.
>
> Ms Rita, Year 1 teacher, Sawrella School

> I see girls as focused and determined . . . more precise. Girls want to obey, and boys are scruffy. Boys don't listen to what others have to say. They have a different mentality.
>
> Ms Lara, parent, Awwista School

> Generally, girls write more in Years 4, 5 and 6. . . even if you find a creative boy, he does it in a hurry, or he writes messily, it does not come from his heart.
>
> Mr Mario, Head of School, Sawrella School

In contrast, a few stakeholders positioned girls as inferior to boys in schooled early literacy. For example, one teacher respondent to the online questionnaire stated that 'boys love writing more than girls'. Most parents pointed out that young boys at home do 'not care about neatness in writing' while young girls' handwriting is 'impeccable' and that the attention of girls during literacy tasks 'is much better'. Other stakeholders' accounts included phrases grounded in the binary framed 'rough boys' and the 'prim and proper girls' stereotypical behaviours in early literacy tasks. Similarly, literature shows how social discourses have informed pedagogy, constrained learner agency (Blair, 2009) and positioned some learners as less 'good' than their peers due to constructed ideologies of the 'ideal learner' (Bradbury, 2013; Jones, 2005). From a feminist poststructural framework, some scholars claim that the constructed stereotype of girls as the 'successful' learners may position them as the 'invisible' learners within classrooms, increasing the likelihood that the needs of disengaged or underachieving girls are overlooked (Charleton et al., 2007; Jones, 2005; Myers, 2000). Taken-for-granted inherited dominant gendered discourses cut both ways. Findings from this study support the arguments put forward by several scholars who attest that dominant hegemonic claims could influence boys' literate identities, and how they view themselves as readers and writers in future years (Fine, 2010; Millard, 1997).

Accepted truths and power relations in schooled early literacy within a Maltese state school scenario

As Figure 2.5 succinctly shows, the cultural backdrop in the context of 21st-century Maltese state schools tends to be constituting a site for boys' disempowerment and girls' empowerment in schooled early literacy learning. Findings suggest that some young boys were recurrently positioned, by a dominated female workforce, in relation to a construct of the dominant 'ideal pupil' (Becker, 1952) as essentially female (quiet, compliant and more 'able' Year 1 learner). How masculinity is understood in a Maltese postcolonial context shapes the discourses of stakeholders within the early years sector account for 'masculinity' in early literacy education today. This is not in line with Article 2 of the UNCRC, where it is stipulated that all children need to be treated and empowered in the same way, also when it comes to early literacy learning. It is apt to ask: How can such dominant discourses of masculinity within a postcolonial context constitute a new space in which discourses on disempowered boys in early literacy can be dismantled and negotiated?

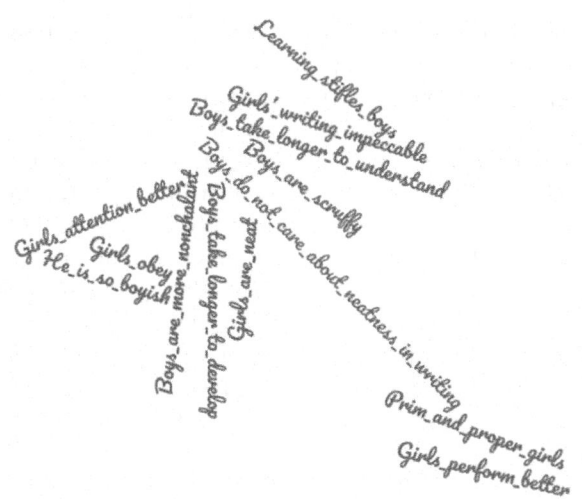

Figure 2.5 A snapshot of the most prominent accepted socially constructed masculinities and femininities in relation to schooled early literacy learning in a Maltese state school scenario

Source: Image created by wordclouds.co.uk

Findings from this study suggest that literacy practice is narrowly perceived as a set of skills to be mastered. The autonomous view (Street, 1984), or the worldview of essentialism, continues to promote binary constructs of gender in early literacy learning. We see this perspective of an agonistic (Freire, 1970) gender and literacy world in the participants' claims favouring the girls' 'neatness' in writing. This evidence transpires dominant perspectives of one group (girls) over another (boys), rooted in a prioritisation of the conventional aspects of writing rather than the meaning and purpose of writing in 21st-century early literacy learning. Findings question equity in the traditional formal approach to early writing instruction mainly grounded in the value given to transcriptional skills (e.g., handwriting, letter formation etc.) and how this is ultimately impacting the constructions of boys' literate identities within a Maltese culture. What would boys' future attitudes towards writing be if they experience schooled literacy practices that make them believe that their writing is 'slow' and 'messy'?

The majority of stakeholders' accepted truths about boys and literacy do not fit in with the belief that there are multiple ways of being literate in social practice as presented by the field of new literacy studies (Gee, 1991; Pahl & Rowsell, 2005) and Street's (1984) 'ideological' model of literacy education. Viewing gender as a binary construct and literacy as a one-size-fits-all, skills-based approach seems to have a connotation with the way gender relations and discourse are produced by adult stakeholders in the context under scrutiny, which may allude to hegemonic masculinities that are toxic to some young boys. Similarly, local and international literature on gender, language and literacy argues the ways in which boys may refuse speaking one language in a bilingual Maltese postcolonial context (Portelli, 2006) or engage in schooled literacy due to ways in which masculinities have been recognised within specific cultures and contexts (Millard, 1997). Critical literacy plays a major role here, as both boys and girls may benefit from the opportunity to interrogate preconceived hegemonic ideas of schooled literacy learning (Charles, 2007). I would add that this needs to happen from the earliest years and with all stakeholders involved through a systemic approach, particularly in contexts like Malta that hold onto a legacy of a highly traditional approach to early literacy.

A critical perspective to hierarchical power structures features in Foucault's (1977) work, as he uses poststructural analyses to challenge accepted truths that reinforce dominance in power relations. This French philosopher suggested that dominant discourses are used as a means to use power and knowledge as a form of social control over the colonised. The exposed power dichotomies between the 'abnormal' boys and the 'normal' girls in schooled early literacy echo a similar power struggle during colonial times in Malta – between the colonisers and the colonised. Thus, it is important that stakeholders in diverse ECEC contexts are mindful of such lingering historical power relations and how these may insistently filter through 21st-century schooled literacy practice. Under the category of protection rights, children have the right to be safe from discrimination (Article 2, United Nations, 1989). Also, Article 28 highlights the right to education grounded in equal opportunity (United Nations, 1989). The understanding and awareness of children's rights as citizens may act as a counter-colonial response in contexts such as Malta. As Lange (2016, p. 5) claims, consciousness is the basis of gender:

> Gender and consciousness in their entanglements are understood and handled together as intersectional categories which have previously been thought separately . . . consciousness is analyzed in transformative interplay with citizenship awareness, whereby citizenship awareness is conceived as a dimension of consciousness.

Early literacy learning, in postcolonial Malta, needs to be liberated, as understood by Freire (1970), in order to establish more socially just, equitable and democratic literacy pedagogies. Through a postcolonial lens, decolonising discourse encourages the rethinking of Eurocentric perspectives to eliminate their credibility. This is in line with Freire's (1970) concept of education as liberation from oppression through 'conscientization'. Early childhood professionals and other stakeholders in ECEC need to reflect and evaluate through a process Freire calls 'conscientization' where individuals examine their views and priviliges and take action for change (Soto, 2010). This form of critical action is key to initiate the path towards a decolonised literacy education in a context that holds on to hierarchical power relation in its discourse, placing young boys in an inferior position in schooled early literacy. Findings from this study imply that children, educators and parents need to exercise critical consciousness through dialogical-relational pedagogy (Freire, 1970) and overcome dominant ideologies that mould their perceptions of gender and early literacy learning. It can be argued that hidden gendered perceptions may hold on to a discriminatory gender stereotype paralysis within postcolonial schooled early literacy learning. If we want to offer brighter and non-discriminatory literacy beginnings for all children (Article 2, United Nations, 1989), it is necessary to create spaces where stakeholders can reflect, act and decolonise the dominant notions of hegemonic masculinities and femininities in schooled early literacy within a Maltese postcolonial context and beyond. Deconstruction of relations of power and knowledge production need to be integrated in new spaces and not create further binarisms.

Challenging popular explanations for the gender gap in literacy achievement within a Maltese state school scenario

It is good to note, however, that some stakeholders drew on a range of explanations and offered a comprehensive perspective throughout. An interesting finding from this enquiry was that a minority of stakeholders challenged existing evidence on the popular rhetoric and existing evidence that underpins the homogeneous claim of boys' underachievement in literacy. They viewed gender as socially constructed and that there are no differences between the sexes in relation to literacy:

> During my years of teaching, I never noted any differences between the sexes. Gender was never an issue of success.
>
> Ms Lina, Head of School, Awwista School

These findings indicated that a minority of stakeholders might not be viewing boys or girls as a homogeneous group as they clearly acknowledged the diversity and needs of every child irrespective of their gender and performance in literacy. This was particularly evident in other comments, such as 'misconception' and 'studies like this and society are passing on the notion that boys are different in learning to read and write'. It can be argued that in conceptualising boys' underachievement broadly, some stakeholders were able to view boys as readers, writers and achievers, and the failing boys and literacy agenda as a phenomenon that could be challenged. In other words, a minority of participants did not view gender as two separate categories but as socially constructed through traditional gender discourses and practices grounded in different schools, social classes and cultures. These findings are a ray of light in postcolonial education, yet the overall findings imply a longstanding need for the decolonisation of early literacy education within a Maltese context. With Reyes and Torres (2007), I view the 'decolonisation of social practices as a re-vision of post-colonialism, based on Freire's philosophy of life and education'. To decolonise literacy education from oppressing conditions in Maltese schools, postcolonialism needs to be revised through decolonised methodologies (e.g., critical literacy, socially just pedagogies, co-constructed curricula and culture circles) in teacher pedagogy, teacher education, professional development for all stakeholders in education and family literacy programmes (Freire, 1970; Reyes & Torres, 2007). A legacy of hierarchical gendered discourse needs to be liberated from oppression through collective action.

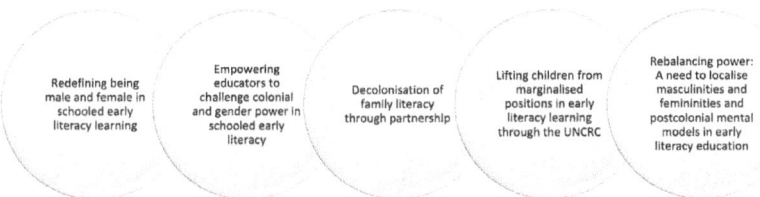

Figure 2.6 The five key takeaways emanating from the stakeholders' discourse grounded in popular explanations for the gender gap in literacy achievement within a Maltese state school scenario

Key takeaways

This chapter concludes with five key takeaways (see Figure 2.6). Each takeaway is unpacked and framed within Freire's (1973) concept of praxis as an invitation to reimagine and hopefully create change through the process of reflection and action.

■ *Redefining being male and female in schooled early literacy learning*
   Reflection: There is a need for children, educators, families and other stakeholders, to explore what it means to be male and female and the intertwining of power relations within their contexts. As this case study shows, an old-fashioned socially constructed gendered power is portraying young boys as powerless in early literacy learning within a postcolonial small island state. Boys, at any age, are not perceived as a uniform group of individuals who are outperformed by girls in literacy practice. National and international literacy testing should stop comparing groups of boys with groups of girls as these popular texts are continuing to promote colonial thinking, unequal power relations and binarisms in the global and local fields of gender and literacy.
   Action: This chapter invites all stakeholders to challenge inherited reproduced power order talk and deficit thinking about males and females in early literacy and generate anti-discriminatory (Article 2, United Nations, 1989) gender discourses and practices grounded in fairness and equal power (MacNaughton, 2000). ECEC needs new spaces to develop praxis (Freire, 1970) for ongoing dialogue, reflection and action to gradually shift the competitive focus on the separate groups of boys and girls in literacy achievement. Stakeholders need to

question who is benefiting from the discourses, interactions and early literacy pedagogies taking place in diverse contexts.

■ *Empowering educators to challenge colonial and gender power in schooled early literacy*
Reflection: It is important that young children's relationships and well-being are regarded by avoiding the risk of having educators that make incorrect assumptions about male learners, deliver negative feedback or treat children unequally. Educators need to be always open to new ideas, and they need to question and challenge the political and social oppression that filters down to their classrooms. What decolonising methodologies can be used to reverse the dominant gendered discourse in postcolonial ECEC contexts?
Action: Educators need to reject gender dualisms in literacy education. They need to engage in critical literacy (Freire, 1985) to construct literacy as social practice and feel empowered to respond to the changing nature of all children's out-of-school literacy practices. Dyer (2020) indicates that educators need opportunities to unpack the concept of conscientisation evolving from Freire's theory of liberation to transform and create change. The deconstruction and critique (Surtees, 2008) of hegemonic discourses and the examination of the 'effects of power' through dialogue and reflective assignments (Sumsion, 2005, p. 196) may be further supported in pre-service ECEC and in-service professional development programmes.

■ *Decolonisation of family literacy through partnership*
Reflection: In early years settings, families are often treated as passive recipients of knowledge within colonising practices that are framed with a top-down curricular perspective. In view of the reported findings, it is important that families are viewed as partners in the early literacy journeys of their children, enabling them to experience the process of conscientisation to resist discriminatory early literacy practice within home and school cultures.
Action: Families in postcolonial ECEC contexts need more occasions to gain collective power that reshapes and recreates dominant gender ideologies within early literacy curricula and practices. A strategy that can be used is Freire's pedagogy of 'culture circles'; a Freiran approach to family literacy that works towards social justice. Research shows (Reyes & Torres, 2007) that this strategy promotes conscientisation and is underpinned by democratic participation and relational pedagogy to co-construct a culturally relevant and socially responsive curriculum. It embraces compromised collective action

to create change. In the implemented relational pedagogy, participants are in a vulnerable position, free to express themselves and to level the playing field of power and knowledge within the ongoing relationships.

■ *Lifting children from marginalised positions in early literacy learning through the UNCRC*
Reflection: There is a need for a conceptualisation of marginality that seeks to unveil and challenge the socio historical processes of power in gender and literacy education. Findings suggest that in a Maltese context, direct critical actions are needed to decolonise gendered discourse in early literacy education and avoid the risk of marginalising boys. Contexts similar to Malta need critical activism for social justice within social power relations in early literacy learning (Pacini-Ketchabaw & Prochner, 2013).

Action: The UNCRC needs to be reconceptualised so that its power may be used in ways that address inequalities in gender and early literacy education. Increasing the awareness and respect towards the UNCRC, and using it as a tool to challenge legacies of gender binarisms in early literacy, may lift children from a marginalised position to the centre of literacy practice, policies and curricula in ECEC contexts. In early childhood settings and schools, all boys and girls need to be recognised as human beings with rights, so that they can be perceived as equally capable and competent for their contributions in families, schools and society at large. Critical activism is required to counter power relations in the fields of gender, literacy and ECEC.

■ *Rebalancing power: A need to localise masculinities and femininities and postcolonial mental models in early literacy education*
Reflection: How masculinities and femininities are negotiated by children in 21st-century early literacy practices, in school and in home cultures across diverse contexts, warrants further examination. More research is needed to explore and identify socially constructed masculinities and femininities and postcolonial mental models in early literacy education.

Action: This chapter calls for future research to investigate unexamined gender configurations, and how these connect with educational systems, policy and practice. If we need to rebalance power in gender and literacy, we need to better understand how boys and girls are experiencing literacy within diverse ECEC contexts. Policymakers and several stakeholders in education need evidence that makes visible the social constructions of masculinities and femininities and postcolonial mental models in early literacy to create change and rethink what is currently taken for granted.

This chapter is an invitation to education stakeholders in diverse contexts to co-create opportunities with other stakeholders to liberate early literacy education from asymmetrical power relations and oppression. It is hoped that the presented findings help in inspiring stakeholders in education and researchers to lead to new ways of thinking that steer away from acknowledging boys' and girls' literacy in traditional binary frameworks (in this case, empowering girls), and critique and address buried sociohistorical inequities within new spaces that allow for dialogue, discourse and interactions through deconstructive action (Sherry & Whitty, 2013). This rethinking followed by critical action cannot certainly take place if the existing evidence and popular discourses on boys, underachievement is opportunely looked at through a constricted view – one that offers explanations, such as those related to biological and role model theory or by looking back at traditional socially constructed masculinities that reinforce gender binarism in the literacy agenda. Doing so will only sustain inequity and difference (Article 2, United Nations, 1989) and there is no time to lose.

In this chapter, the dual lens of children's rights and postcolonial theory brings forth a nuanced perspective that may be utilised to address past and present sociopolitical and sociohistorical power relations in the fields of gender, literacy and ECEC. Thus, I argue that increased awareness of postcolonial and children's rights perspectives may assist in the creation of new spaces for 'conscientization' (Freire, 1970) to develop a shared view of social change to challenge and critique tacit legacies of essentialist worldviews and hierarchical gender binarisms in early literacy learning. The next chapter seeks to unfold early literacy learning through five- to six-year-old boys' eyes.

Notes

1 The term 'discourse' in this book is understood as 'ways of knowing and doing' as defined in Pacini-Ketchabaw and Prochner (2013).
2 'Gender responsiveness' refers to the outcomes that reflect an understanding of gender roles and inequalities and which make an effort to encourage equal participation and equal and fair distribution of benefits. Gender responsiveness is accomplished through gender analysis and gender inclusiveness.

References

Alloway, N., Freebody, P., Gilber, P., & Muspratt, S. (2002). *Boys, literacy and schooling: Expanding the repertoires of practice*. J.S. McMillan Printing Group.

Becker, H. S. (1952). Social class variation in the teacher-pupil relationship. *Journal of Educational Sociology, 25*, 451–465.

Biddulph, S. (1997). *Raising boys.* Thorsons.

Blair, D. (2009). Learner agency: To understand & be understood. *British Journal of Music Education, 26*(2), 173–187.

Bloch, M. (1992). Critical perspectives on the historical relationship between child development and early childhood education research. In S. A. Kessler & B. B. Swadener (Eds.), *Reconceptualizing the early childhood curriculum: Beginning the dialogue* (pp. 3–20). Teachers College Press.

Bradbury, A. (2013). Education policy and the 'ideal learner': Producing recognisable learner-subjects through early years assessment. *British Journal of Sociology of Education, 34*(1), 1–19.

Brooker, L. (2005). Learning to Be a Child: cultural diversity and early years ideology. In N. Yelland (Ed.) *Critical Issues in Early Childhood Education* (pp. 115–130). New York: Open University Press.

Brownhill, S. (2016). Male role models in education-based settings (0–8): An english perspective . In S. Brownhill, J. Warin, & I. Wernersson (Eds.), *Men, masculinities and teaching in early childhood education: International perspectives on gender and care* (pp. 26–35). Routledge.

Cannella, G. S. (1997). *Deconstructing early childhood education: Social justice and revolution.* Peter Lang.

Cannella, G. S., & Viruru, R. (2004). *Childhood and (post-colonization): Power, education and contemporary practice.* Routledge.

Charles, C. (2007). Exploring "girl power": Gender, literacy and the textual practices of young women attending an elite school. *English Teaching: Practice and Critique, 6*(2), 72–88. http://education.waikato.ac.nz/research/files/etpc/2007v6n2art5.

Charleton, E., Mills, M., Martino, W., & Beckett, L. (2007). Sacrificial girls: A case study of the impact of streaming and setting on gender reform. *British Education Research Journal, 33*, 459–478.

Cigman, J. (2014). *Supporting boys' writing in the early years.* Routledge.

Claxton, G. (2008). *What's the point of school?* Oneworld Publications.

Connolly, P. (2004). *Boys and schooling in the early years.* Routledge.

Dahlberg, G., Moss, P., & Pence, A. (2007). *Beyond quality in early childhood education and care: Languages of evaluation.* Routledge.

Dent, M. (2017, December 15). *Getting little ones ready for big school.* www.maggiedent.com/blog/getting-little-ones-ready-big-school/.

Dyer, M. (2020). Critical literacy: Promoting equity in early childhood settings. *He Kupu the Word, 6*(3), 34–40.

Evans, L., & Davies, K. (2000). No sissy boys here: A content analysis of the representation of masculinity in elementary school reading textbooks. *Sex Roles, 42*(3), 255–270.

Fine, C. (2010). *Delusions of gender.* W.W. Norton.

Foucault, M. (1977). *Discipline and punish: The birth of prison.* Pantheon.

Francis, B. (2008). Teaching manfully? Exploring gendered subjectivities and power via analysis of men teachers' gender performance. *Gender and Education, 20*(2), 109–122.

Freire, P. (1970). *Pedagogy of the oppressed.* New York: Seabury Press.

Freire, P. (1973). *Education for critical consciousness.* Seabury.

Freire, P. (1985). Reading the world and reading the word: An interview with Paolo Freire. *Language Arts, 62*(1), 15–21.

Gee, J. P. (1991). *Social linguistics: Ideology in discourses.* Falmer Press.

Gurian, M. (2001). *Boys and girls learn differently.* Jossey-Bass.

Hempel-Jorgensen, A. (2009). The construction of the 'ideal pupil' and pupils' perceptions of 'misbehaviour' and discipline: Contrasting experiences from a low-socio-economic and high-socio-economic primary school. *British Journal of Sociology of Education, 30*(4), 435–448.

Hempel-Jorgensen, A. (2015). Learner agency and social justice: What can creative pedagogy contribute to socially just pedagogies? *Pedagogy, Culture & Society, 23*(4), 531–554.

Hempel-Jorgensen, A., Cremin, T., Harris, D., & Chamberlain, L. (2017). *Understanding boys' (dis)engagement with reading for pleasure: Project findings.* The Open University. http://oro.open.ac.uk/49310/1/BA%20RfP%20report%20to%20funder.pdf.

Heyman, G. D., & Legare, C. H. (2004). Children's beliefs about gender differences in the academic and social domains. *Sex Roles, 50*(3), 227–239. https://doi.org/10.1023/B:SERS.0000015554.12336.30

Hyland, N. E. (2010). Social justice in early childhood classrooms: What the research tells us. *Young Children,* 82–87.

Jones, S. (2005). The invisibility of the underachieving girl. *International Journal of Inclusive Education, 9,* 269–286.

Laevers, F., & Verboven, L. (2000). Gender related role patterns in preschool settings. Can 'experiential education' make a difference? *European Early Childhood Education Research Journal, 8*(1), 25–42. https://doi.org/10.1080/13502930085208471

Lange, D. (2016). Foreword. In N. Barongo-Muweke (Ed.), *Decolonizing education: Towards reconstructing a theory of citizenship education for postcolonial Africa* (pp. 5–7). Springer.

Langford, R. (2010). Critiquing child-centred pedagogy to bring children and early childhood educators into the centre of a democratic pedagogy. *Contemporary Issues in Early Childhood, 11,* 113–127.

Lubeck, S. (1985). *Sandbox society: Early education in black and white America.* Falmer Press.

Lubeck, S. (1994). The politics of developmentally appropriate practice. In B. Mallory & R. New (Eds.), *Diversity and developmentally appropriate practices* (pp. 17–43). Teachers College Press.

MacNaughton, G. (2000). *Rethinking gender in early childhood education.* Allen & Ulwin.

Martino, W. (2008). Male teachers as role models: Addressing issues of masculinity, pedagogy and the re-masculinization of schooling. *Curriculum Inquiry, 38*(2), 189–221.

Master, A., Cheryan, S., Moscatelli, S., & Melzoff, A. N. (2017). Programming experience promotes higher STEM motivation among first-grade girls. *Journal of Experimental Child Psychology, 160*, 92–106. https://doi.org/10.1016/j.jecp.2017.03.013

Matějů, P., & Smith, M. L. (2015). Are boys that bad? Gender gaps in measured skills, grades and aspirations in Czech elementary schools. *British Journal of Sociology of Education, 36*, 871–895.

McLaren, P. (2002). Critical pedagogy: A look at the major concepts. In A. E. A. Darder (Ed.), *The critical pedagogy reader* (pp. 69–96). Routledge/Falmer.

Mifsud, C. (2000). *Literacy and education in a changing world in libraries and national development.* Paper presented at the Proceedings of a Conference Organized by the Għaqda Bibljotekarji (Library Association, Malta).

Mifsud, C. L., Grech, R., Hutchison, D., Morrison, J., Rudd, P., & Hanson, J. (2004). *Literacy for school improvement: Value added for Malta.* Agenda Publishers.

Millard, E. (1997). Differently literate: Gender identity and the construction of the developing reader. *Gender and Education, 9*(1), 31–48.

Ministry for Education and Employment [MEDE]. (2013). *2009+ programme for international student assessment [PISA] Malta report.* https://researchand innovation.gov.mt/en/Documents/PISA%202009+%20Malta%20Report.pdf

Mulvey, K. L., & Killen, M. (2015). Challenging gender stereotypes: Resistance and exclusion. *Child Development, 86*(3), 681–694. https://doi.org/10.1111/cdev.12317

Myers, K. (2000). *Whatever happened to equal opportunities in schools? Gender equality initiatives in education.* Open University Press.

Organisation for Economic Co-operation and Development (OECD). (2018). *Starting strong: Early childhood education and care.* Author.

Pacini-Ketchabaw, V., & Prochner, L. (2013). *Re-situating Canadian early childhood education.* Peter Lang.

Pennycook, J. (2011). (RE)engendering classroom space: Teachers, curriculum policy, and boys' literacy. *Language and Literacy, 13*(2), 9–22.

Perry, D. G., Pauletti, R. E., & Cooper, P. J. (2019). Gender identity in childhood: A review of the literature. *International Journal of Behavioral Development, 43*(4), 289–304. https://doi.org/10.1177/0165025418811129

Pollack, W. (1998). *Real boys: Rescuing our sons from the myths of boyhood.* Random House.

Portelli, J. (2006). Language: An important signifier of masculinity in a bilingual context. *Gender and Education, 18*(4), 413–430.

Reyes, L. V., & Torres, M. N. (2007). Decolonizing family literacy in a culture circle: Reinventing the family literacy educator's role. *Journal of Early Childhood Literacy, 7*(1), 73–94. https://doi.org/10.1177/1468798407074837.

Rowe, K. J. (2001). *Equal and different? Yes, but what really matters.* Paper presented at the Background Paper to Keynote Address Presented to the Joint Conference of the Alliance of Girls' Schools Australasia and the International Boys' Schools Coalition.

Saukko, P. (2003). Combining methodologies in cultural studies. In P. Saukko (Ed.), *Doing research in cultural studies: An introduction to classical and new methodological approaches* (pp. 11–35). SAGE.

Shallwani, S. (2010). Racism and imperialism in the child development discourse: Deconstructing "developmentally appropriate practice". In S. G. Cannella & D. L. Soto (Eds.), *Childhood: A handbook* (pp. 214–231). Peter Lang.

Sherry, R., & Whitty, P. (2013). Valuing subjective complexities: Disrupting the tyranny of time. In V. Pacini-Ketchabaw & L. Prochner (Eds.), *Re-situating Canadian early childhood education*. Peter Lang.

Skolverket. (2006). *Gender differences in goal fulfilment and education choices.* Tabergs Printing. www.skolverket.se/download/18.6bfaca41169863e6a65648a/1553959642986/pdf1775.pdf

Smyth, E. (2007). Gender and education. In R. Teese, S. Lamb, & M. Duru-Bellat (Eds.), *International studies in educational inequality, theory and policy: Educational inequality: Persistence and change* (pp. 135–154). Springer.

Sommers, C. H. (2000). *The war against boys: How misguided feminism is harming our young men.* Simon & Schuster.

Soto, L. D. (2010). Constructing critical futures: Projects from the heart. In G. S. Cannella & L. D. Soto (Eds.), *Childhood: A handbook* (pp. 375–380). Peter Lang.

Street, B. V. (1984). *Literacy in theory and practice.* Cambridge University Press.

Sumsion, J. (2005). Putting postmodern theories into practice in early childhood teacher education. In S. Ryan & S. Grieshaber (Eds.), *Practical transformation and transformational practices: Globalization, postmodernism, and early childhood education* (pp. 193–216). Elsevier.

Surtees, N. (2008). Teachers following children? Heteronormative responses within a discourse of child-centredness and the emergent curriculum. *Australian Journal of Early Childhood, 33*(3), 10–17.

United Nations. (1989). *Convention on the rights of the child.* https://www2.ohchr.org/english/bodies/crc/docs/AdvanceVersions/GeneralComment7Rev1.pdf.

United Nations Development Programme (UNDP). (2015). *Gender responsive national communications toolkit.* Phoenix Design Aid A/S.

Viruru, R. (2001). *Early childhood education: Postcolonial perspectives from India.* SAGE.

Viruru, R. (2005). The impact of postcolonial theory on early childhood education. *Journal of Education, 35*, 7–30.

Warson-Williams, C., & Riddell, A. (2011). *Masculinity and educational performance: Engaging our boys in the classroom.* Paper presented at the Summary Prepared for USAID and the Jamaica Partners for Educational Progress, EduExchange E-Discussion. www.mona.uwi.edu/cop/sites/default/files/consolidated_reply_files/EduExcha nge_Summary_3_Final_0.pdf.

Yelland, N. (1998). *Gender in early childhood.* Routledge.

Younger, M., & Cobbett, M. (2014). Gendered perceptions of schooling: Classroom dynamics and inequalities within four caribbean secondary schools. *Educational Review, 66*, 1–21.

Younger, M., Warrington, M., & Williams, J. (1999). The gender gap and classroom interactions: Reality and rhetoric? *British Journal of Sociology of Education, 20*, 325–341.

Zambo, D., & Brozo, W. G. (2009). *Bright beginnings for boys: Engaging young boys in active literacy*. International Reading Association.

3 'I get bored'

Beating boredom through boys' views on a highly formalised approach to early literacy

Chapter Overview

This chapter re-examines five-to six-year-old boys' views on a highly formalised approach to early literacy learning within three Maltese state schools through a dual lens of children's rights and postcolonial theory. It draws on the highpoint of my doctoral project (Bonello, 2018) – the young boys' voices – and a subsequent publication inspired by the same (Bonello, 2021). The chapter uncovers how early literacy pedagogic practices in a Maltese ECEC postcolonial context are shaping boys' understandings of what constitutes the process of learning to read and write. The boys' views were collected through three focus group interviews conducted in three Maltese state schools. The presented findings strongly indicate that highly formalised schooled literacy practices may demotivate some young boys from developing confidence and motivation to read and write. Thus, building on Freire's (1970) concept of 'banking education', it is argued that schooled literacy in a Maltese postcolonial early years environment may continue to colonise young minds if we do not listen to what young children have to say. In conclusion, five key takeaways are presented for stakeholders in education to rethink and reimagine the teaching of early reading and writing tied to the inherited legacies of a colonial mindset, and gain a deeper understanding of how children's rights may assist in beating the boredom in early literacy education.

DOI: 10.4324/9781003125525-3

Through the lens of an oppressed educator: A commitment to empower young boys' voices

As an early childhood educator, I have experienced moments where I wanted change to happen but felt helpless. I witnessed different forms of established forces or barriers derived from educational policy and systems that made me act in ways that were not in line with the theory and teaching philosophy that I acquired and subscribed to. Through my experience in a Maltese education system, I often experienced boys who were unmotivated, despondent and not keen to participate in reading and writing tasks, forced to fill in workbooks and worksheets from the age of five and hesitatingly being identified and pulled out of their classrooms to undertake a phonics test in a separate room. I was also told that there was something wrong with my teaching when five-year-olds did not pass the phonics tests in English and Maltese (after three months in Year 1 – the first year of compulsory schooling in Malta). The children who did not pass such tests were labelled as having 'literacy difficulties', and had to attend literacy pull-out sessions in smaller groups in another classroom. Thus, given my theoretical and practical background in the field of ECEC, which eventually developed into critical activism for social justice in the early years, I started questioning the one-size-fits-all early literacy tests grounded in the knowledge bases of child development and developmental psychology. In this light, Curry and Cannella (2013) point out that:

> Universalist foundational assumptions include an acceptance of an adult-child dichotomy that privileges those who are older; progress as a necessity of the human condition both individually and as a species; and a one-size-fits-all linear, developmental, predetermined sequence model for human functioning. As an example, when a defined form of progress does not occur, the individual (most often one categorised as "child") is labelled as deficient. Child development assumptions have led to social and cultural injustices, which in turn have limited life possibilities for those who are younger by creating (1) multiple forms of privilege and control, (2) covert methods for social regulation and domination, (3) an acceptance of hierarchical/patriarchal human relations, and (4) views of humanity as deficient.

As an educator in Maltese schools, I felt the pressure of being bound to a system where universalist, child development, and child psychological perspectives continued to promote the reproduction of colonialism in early literacy pedagogy. In other words, I have lived how this led to a continued attempt to divide and classify young children as having literacy difficulties in reading and writing or being early readers and writers – the 'ideal' state of the ideal child who is 'well-prepared' for formal schooling at the age of five. Some young children did pass the Maltese and English phonics tests with flying colours. Yet, I have a vivid memory of one of the five-year-old boys who found this test easy because he already knew the letter sounds and how to read fluently from the beginning of the scholastic year. By time, I noted that his motivation to read and write switched off when he was introduced to a one-size-fits-all systematic synthetic phonics (SSP) programme in Year 1. For example, when engaged in such practice he used to repeat the same word with a sad tone: 'Boring!'. And he was not the only one; something needed to be done. I tried to change this view of rigid early literacy learning by requesting permission to implement a balanced literacy approach in Years 1, 2 and 3 (five- to eight-year-olds) – underpinned by a progressive education philosophy. This approach, promoted in the National Literacy Strategy (NLS) (MEDE, 2014), increased the boys' power and agency as they experienced more authentic reading and writing practices. For example, writing had a meaningful purpose and a clear audience, it was not dictated through pre-set titles or dominantly co-authored by adults.

The contrasting influences these different approaches to literacy education had on the young made me realise that socially unjust educational practices cannot remain hidden behind closed classroom doors. The neoliberal, market-driven (Pratt, 2016; Sims, 2017; Rogers et al., 2020) literacy education systems that give precedence to myriad resources for the teaching of reading and writing across most church, state and independent schools in Malta, continues to promote a linear approach to early literacy learning. I was, and still am, witnessing and living the pressure of high-stakes testing in a postcolonial Maltese education system and how it filters top-down in Maltese ECEC, sustaining a sense of being held by the oppressor and embracing conformity in literacy education. These short vignettes and similar personal experiences, as a mother of two boys and a sister of three, helped me reflect and served as the trigger to a question that haunted me and eventually bound me with committing to having young boys in Maltese schools participating in the reported broader doctoral project: Would the power of young boys' views on their schooled literacy experiences become the starting point of change in highly formalised approaches to early literacy within Maltese schools?

Previous research has pointed out that children's perspectives on the quality of the education they receive are rarely investigated (Cook-Sather, 2002; Einarsdottir, 2005). Lansdown (2004, p. 4) states that young children have been less seen as participants in research than children over the age of eight, and thus explains that the UNCRC

> extends participation rights to all children capable of expressing a view. It embodies no age restrictions. There is a pressing need, therefore, to explore approaches which address the rights of younger children to participate, and in so doing, to review the culture, attitudes and practices prevailing in those environments where young children spend their time.

So far, no attention has been devoted to unpacking the concept of boys' underachievement in literacy attainment through young boys' views on their experience of reading and writing in a formal educational environment, and examining the outcome through a children's rights and postcolonial lens. This chapter attempts to fill this gap. It particularly seeks to better understand schooled early literacy pedagogy through the perspectives of the young boys in a context where formal schooling starts at the age of five. Additionally, Chapter 3 traces the lasting and continued colonial influence, and examines how a children's rights perspective features in the young boys' views on their lived schooled reading and writing practices in Malta. The refocusing of the theoretical lens, from the doctoral journey to this book, served as a bridge to further strengthen the arguments developed in previous publications – my doctoral thesis (Bonello, 2018) and the two papers that followed (Bonello, 2019, 2021).

Seeing reading and writing in a postcolonial Maltese ECEC context with boys' eyes

The participation of the boys in this case study was presented to them as a right (United Nations, 1989) to safeguard this study from being categorised as an inquiry where young children are silenced. In this section, I will provide a re-examination of the findings emerging from the participation of fourteen five- to six-year-old boys in three separate focus groups conducted in three Maltese state schools (see Chapter 1). It draws on some of the data that was categorised into themes following a thematic analysis of the young boys' and other stakeholders focus groups and interviews in the broader doctoral work. In this chapter, a summary of the key findings that relate to the boys' perspectives will be presented in two main separate sub-sections:

1 The young boys' views on schooled reading practices
2 The young boys' views on schooled writing practices

In both sub-sections, the discussion will be grounded in the different ways five- to six-year-old boys looked at schooled reading and writing in 2017 in a Maltese ECEC context, and how these lived experiences feature in the significant dual lens of children's rights and postcolonial theory. The boys' views presented in this chapter portray an overall summary of the three focus groups' discussions.

The young boys' views on schooled reading practice

There is no end in sight for the controversial debates on how and when reading should be taught in the early years. Similarly, the concern on the gender gap in literacy attainment continues to surface on a global level. If such debates revolve around the literacy education of young children, and the literacy achievement of some boys, why do we not ask them in the first place? What models of literacy nurtures boys' motivation and positive learning dispositions to read and write from their earliest years?

The young boys' views on systematic synthetic phonics (SSP) instruction

In the three Maltese state schools, the boys experienced the teaching of reading through SSP programmes. This means that the reading instruction they experienced placed more emphasis on the explicit and systematic teaching of letter-sound correspondence rather than the contrasting whole language approach where the focus is on the meaning of words in meaningful contexts (i.e., letter-sound relationships are taught incidentally). During the focus groups, the boys were shown pictures of the flashcards used during the daily drilling exercises which focused on the links between graphemes-phonemes/letters-sounds. They were also shown pictures of their classroom interactive whiteboard which was used to show them an image of, for example, a three-letter word for blending: 'd-a-m = dam'. The boys had to produce each letter sound and then blend them, repeating after their teacher. Most of the five- to six-year-old boys in the three schools pointed to the sad face on the emotion card:

A me non piace perché dobbiamo ripetere.
I don't like it because we have to repeat.

Carlo

Jien niddejjaq noqgħod nagħmel dawk il-kliem kollha, noqogħdu nitkellmu 's-o-d', u niddejqu ngħidu l-ittri aħna.
I get bored doing all those words, we have to say 's-o-/d', and we get bored saying the letters.

Mark

Most of the comments revealed that the boys' experience with SSP was not meaningful for them. Also, it was surprising to discover that most boys stated that they 'felt sleepy' and their 'eyes hurt' during the time they spent repeating and blending and segmenting letter sounds presented on the interactive whiteboard. Only two boys pointed to a happy face and declared that they feel good during SSP. One boy, named Karl, said, 'I can read the word "rocket" and I like the rocket very much', while another boy, Sam, said, 'I feel happy if I say them all because then the teacher will be proud of me'.

Overall, the boys' reaction to their experiences with SSP programmes echoed the popular adages in the field of education: 'students are not a tabula rasa' and 'students are not empty vessels to be filled with knowledge'. The boys' views on this universal approach to the teaching of reading seemed to fit more in an autonomous model than an ideological model of literacy (Street, 1984). This implies that the SSP instruction they experienced in the early years appeared more grounded in a dominant ideology barring the possibility for the young boys to be co-participants in their experiences of early reading, as well as forcing them to reproduce the knowledge older human beings are transmitting.

Further, the boys' views support the claims made by several scholars who criticise the isolation of a SSP phonics approach to teaching reading (Walsh et al., 2011; Whitehead, 2010) and question the relevance of phonics check tests in ECEC settings (Clark, 2016; Robert-Holmes & Bradbury, 2016). Excessive focus on reading skills reflects a narrow definition of reading as a technical and cognitive skill that overlooks multimodal reading skills (Levy, 2011). This view of reading in 21st-century Maltese early years classrooms is reminiscent of how literacy was perceived during the colonial period, sustaining an unjust power relationship between the older and the younger. Over time, literacy started to be viewed as social practice that also gives voice to children, regarding and respecting them as active citizens with rights (Hernandez-Zamora, 2010). In this light, the International Reading Association (IRA, 2000) issued a set of ten principles (see Table 3.1) that honour children's rights (United Nations, 1989) to excellent reading instruction. These ten principles 'provide a means for evaluating current policy and classroom practice, and a direction for change where it is necessary' (IRA, 2000, p. 4). The Association claims that in the best interest of every child (Article 3, United Nations, 1989) reading programmes should be built on these values (IRA, 2000).

The IRA strongly believes that to honour these rights – that is, to meet our obligation to provide excellent reading instruction to every child – classrooms need to be rethought, sufficient monetary investments must be made and communities must wholeheartedly support reading reform efforts. In this book, I will draw on some of these principles grounded in children's

Table 3.1 Honouring children's rights to excellent reading instruction: A set of comprehensive principles

1	Children have a right to appropriate early reading instruction based on their individual needs
2	Children have a right to reading instruction that builds both skill and the desire to read increasingly complex materials
3	Children have the right to well-prepared teachers who keep their skills up to date through effective professional development
4	Children have the right of access to a wide variety of books and other reading material in the classroom, school and community libraries
5	Children have a right to reading assessment that identifies their strengths as well as their needs and involves them in making decisions about their own learning
6	Children have a right to supplemental instruction from professionals specifically prepared to teach reading
7	Children have a right to reading instruction that involves parents and communities in their academic lives
8	Children have a right to reading instruction that makes meaningful use of their first language skills
9	Children have a right to equal access to the technology used for the improvement of reading instruction
10	Children have a right to classrooms that optimise learning opportunities

Source: International Reading Association (2000)

rights to see how they feature in the boys' responses to the teaching of reading in the reported Maltese case study.

Principle two (see Table 3.1) focuses on children's rights to experience instruction on both the skill and will to read. Findings from the Maltese case study show that the majority of the five- to six-year-old boys were getting bored when reading was experienced through the formal teaching of SSP programmes. This is evident in claims such as 'I get bored', 'I do not like it' or 'I get tired'. These phrases make visible the detrimental and hidden impact on boys' early reading experiences following their exposure to the decontextualised and irrelevant formal teaching of SSP in three Maltese early primary classrooms. It is interesting to note that the boys who pointed at a happy face on the emotion card did not exhibit any sign of excitement in their tone of voice. One of the boys claimed that he feels happy during the SSP repetitive routine with flashcards because if he tells them all the teacher is proud of him. Similarly, in her book on young boys and writing, Cigman (2014) claims that early writing practice is likely to turn into a task done for the teacher if transcriptional skills are prioritised. Sam's comment in this study raises the question of whether the emphasis on SSP instruction makes him view reading as a task that needs to be completed for the teacher to be proud of him. Karl also pointed at a happy face and recognised the card that showed the rocket because it linked to something he experienced outside school, and this made him feel good. It has been well documented that an increase in young children's engagement and motivation in schooled literacy learning is evident when popular culture, play and the continuity between home and school literacy practices are used to provide a meaningful context (Bonello, 2010; Roskos & Christie, 2007; Levy, 2011; Marsh, 2005). The boys' responses take us back to principle one (see Table 3.1) and raise the question: Is the boys' experience of early reading in Maltese context grounded in an approach focused on their individual needs to honour their right to excellent reading instruction? The boys' views above show that honouring children's right to be heard (Articles 12 and 13, United Nations, 1989), amidst the never-ending 'reading wars' (Pearson, 2004), is critical. Children's perspectives offer new spaces for stakeholders in literacy education to critically reflect on schooled early literacy practices.

The educators of these boys relied heavily on SSP programmes due to the English and Maltese textbooks and syllabus they had to cover during Year 1 (i.e., with five- to six-year-olds) and the phonics tests linked to the Core Competence Literacy Checklists (DQSE, 2009). Similarly, in Boardman's (2019) study early years educators prioritised the teaching of phonics in isolation with two-year-olds to ensure that they are conforming with policy, school readiness agenda and assessment pressures dominant in the United Kingdom. As stipulated in the work of Bowers (2020), research in the field of psychology indicates that the reading wars (Pearson, 2004) between phonics and a whole language approach to the teaching of reading are over because SSP is now recognised as a more effective method of the initial teaching of reading (National Reading Panel, 2000; Rowe, 2005; Rose, 2006; Castles et al., 2018). This implies that early reading should focus on the systematic teaching of letter-sound relationships. Conversely, the young boys' opinions from the presented case study do not seem to favour this widespread consensus on SSP as the best approach to initial reading instruction. In his recent systematic review, Bowers (2020) concludes that 'there is little or no evidence that SSP is better than the most common alternative methods used in schools' (p. 682). Consequently, with Bowers (2020, p. 682), and in an attempt to encourage action that takes into account the views of young children (Article 12, United Nations, 1989), I argue that despite the compelling consensus on the teaching of SSP as a better alternative method to whole language approach or balanced literacy in early reading instruction, researchers and policymakers in education should consider alternative socially just approaches – not only for children but also for educators to allow them to meet the needs of all children in their care (Campbell et al., 2014).

The boys' views on classroom books

This section explores how classroom books are perceived by five- to six-year-old boys in three Maltese state schools. Principle number four (see Table 3.1) refers to the children's right to access 'a wide variety of books and other reading material' and this includes the classroom and school environment. Several scholars have strongly suggested that children's interests should be recognised, including boys' interests, to ensure that no child is turned off when it comes to reading (Neu & Weinfield, 2007; Fletcher, 2006; Newkirk, 2002). In the Maltese case study, the boys seemed to favour non-fiction books and other books that matched their interests. However, these were not easily accessible in their classrooms. When the boys were shown pictures of the books they had in the classroom, the majority did not comment positively:

> Jien li għandi d-dar jogħġbuni ta' Batman.
> I like the ones I have at home about Batman.
>
> Paul

> Non mi piaciono i libri della scuola. Lo preso quello di cars a scuola, mi piace. Ci sono altri che non mi piaciono.
> I don't like the books available at school. I took the one about ars from school, I like it. There are some others that I don't like.
>
> Beppe

Luca and Tim were the only two boys that seemed satisfied with the books they had in the classroom and at home:

> Jien inħossni 'happy' għax nista' naqrahom il-kliem.
> I feel happy because I can read the words.
>
> Tim

> I like them both.
>
> Luca

The boys' claims above highlight a need for popular culture, community-specific and culturally relevant texts in the three Year 1 classrooms. The paper-based texts they encountered seemed to be dominated by texts that are not relevant to the boys' out-of-school contexts, and there seemed to be a mismatch with the boys' level of reading ability. The evidence illustrates that most boys in this study were not experiencing their right to a classroom environment that optimises their reading opportunities in terms of skill (due to inappropriate provision of reading texts – 'they're difficult') and desire to read (texts that do not relate to their outside worlds – 'I like the ones I have at home') (IRA, 2000, p. 1, principles one, two and ten).

'New textual landscapes' (Carrington, 2005) were not part of these boys' schooled reading experiences, as the only time they encountered digital texts was when they were blending and segmenting during SSP instruction – looking at letters on the classroom interactive whiteboard. It can be argued that the classroom book texts in these early primary classrooms are not providing all boys with the opportunity to perceive themselves as capable and competent readers, thus barring the affordances of desirable and pleasurable classroom book texts.

In this light, other studies highlighted that extending the gap between home and school literacy experiences for boys increases demotivation and disengagement, leading to reading failure in future years (Alloway, 2007; Rowan et al., 2002; Smith & Wilhelm, 2002). Conversely, other scholars see the promotion of books related to boys' interests as a solution that further promotes gender binaries and biological determinism (Hammet & Sanford, 2008; Martino, 2008). Neu and Weinfield (2007) found that boys generally resist the books suggested by their teachers, and subsequently recommend that teachers should let boys choose their books freely. Literature shows that if media, popular culture and technology are valued in schooled literacy practices, young children's motivation and engagement would increase as their constructed literate identities are acknowledged (Carrington, 2005; Dyson, 1997; Marsh, 2005). Millard and Marsh (2001, p. 37) argue that:

> at a time when literacy practices are changing, both at home and in school, it is imperative that schools examine the materials they provide to ensure that the interests of all children are reflected in the text made available for sharing in the home.

This study suggests that to decolonise the classroom provision of texts there is the need to put the child first by respecting and recognising their worlds. The boys' views show that having less choice in terms of text provision, being silenced and experiencing high expectations of reading and comprehension levels at the age of five, might be jeopardising the nurturing of their innate intrinsic motivation that opens the door to lifelong reading (Griffiths, 2012). In other words, 'A student with skill, may be capable, but without will, she cannot become a reader' (Cambria & Guthrie, 2010, p. 16).

The boys' views on a balanced literacy approach to the teaching of reading

A balanced literacy approach is made up of several components to provide individual, small group, whole group and meaningful literacy activities that reach out to all learners in the early years and beyond (Mermelstein, 2006; Pressley, 2006; Tompkins, 2013). The policy document, *A National Literacy Strategy for All in Malta and Gozo* (MEDE, 2014), proposes and defines 'balanced literacy' as a curricular methodology aimed to integrate the various modalities of literacy instruction to allow children to work at their independent levels of reading and writing with adult support. The document identifies these components as read aloud; modelled writing; interactive writing; shared/guided/independent reading and writing; and word study; and explains that through the combined efforts of children, educators and parents/guardians it will result in a successful learning environment. The boys experienced a limited number of lessons that promoted components of a balanced approach to reading grounded in a more rights-based and child-centred approach. In the reported case study, I witnessed a minority of two episodes (during the three weeks of observation): reading aloud in the classroom and dialogic reading in the outdoor area. Boys from Awwista and Sawrella Schools got excited, and pointed at the happy face on the emotion cards when they were shown these photographs:

> Nieħu gost meta t-'teacher' taqra ktieb!
> I like it when the teacher reads a book!
>
> Zak

The boys expressed their joy and excitement through the tonality of their voices. It was evident they preferred collaborative and child-centred literacy pedagogy embedded in the view of literacy as social practice, which is an ideological model of literacy (Street, 1984). This approach reflects children's rights in literacy education through co-participation and the promotion of learning that is more meaningful to young children. Following this outcome from the three schools concerned, and my past personal experiences in Maltese schools, I think that it is apt to ask: Will highly formalised literacy instruction at the age of five continue to be implemented, or in such a case, will young boys' voices be listened to and taken into account to transform the teaching of reading into a more equitable and rights-based approach for all – thus, acting in children's best interest? (Articles 3, 12 and 13, UNCRC, United Nations, 1989). The boys' views bring up the argument that 21st-century early literacy learning in a Maltese postcolonial context may be reinforcing the injustices of imperialism, and outweighing the efforts and passions of educators who seem to try and infiltrate a literacy curriculum that decolonises the mind. In this light, Wolstein (2017, p. 1) states that:

> In order for students to be successful and prepared for what the future may bring, a reading literacy curriculum needs to be student focused instead of text focused, present multicultural perspectives, utilize both print and digital sources, draw from fiction and non-fiction, offer flexibility, and most importantly, lead students to think and understand deeply. I hypothesize that this deep thinking would be best facilitated by allowing students to see the world through a multiplicity of eyes, instead of just a Western perspective.

Although the National Curriculum Framework (NCF) (MEDE, 2012), the National Literacy Strategy (NLS) (MEDE, 2014) and other national policy documents promote a more child-centred and progressive philosophy for the under-sevens in 21st century Malta, meaningful and contextualised early reading practice seems to be implemented as a one-off activity in early primary state classrooms. This is not surprising given that Maltese education and schooling has for centuries been influenced by different views of children, childhood and reading.

The boys' views on early writing practice

The art of writing is key to success in education and life (Beam & William, 2015). Yet, recent research keeps showing that many children are experiencing a deficiency in writing enjoyment (Clark & Teravainen, 2017). In early years practice, there is the need for the development of a shared understanding of writing as an act of communication that conveys meaningful and enjoyable messages in different ways (Browne, 2008). During the English and Maltese lessons observed, the boys' writing experiences were mainly grounded in the value given to transcriptional skills (e.g., handwriting, letter formation, etc.). The majority of the boys pointed to a sad face on the card when shown pictures of themselves copying from an interactive whiteboard to their lined copybooks using pencils (which was the most common writing practice observed), and claimed that they did not manage to write all the letters in the lines, that their hands hurt or that they feel sad writing. Overall, most five- to six-year-old boys showed a lack of enjoyment when writing:

> Jien niddejjaq nikteb.
> I don't like writing.
>
> Isaac

Only a few boys pointed to a happy face, yet they did not seem enthusiastic about the writing they experienced:

> I am happy for my hands because they are not hurting, because I go faster.
>
> Sam

These boys, as evident above, associated the word 'hurt' with writing. For example, even Zak stated that he enjoys writing but he also mentioned that his 'fingers still hurt'. Similar to the reading practices they experienced, the boys reacted positively to the photograph showing a more meaningful and child-centred approach to early writing. When boys in Awwista School were shown an image featuring them whilst writing letters in Maltese using coloured chalk on black paper, all boys got excited and pointed at a happy face on their cards:

> I like it too because it's messy!
>
> Ben

Overall, the boys' reactions showed that they were more in favour of participatory, child-centred and playful schooled early writing practice embedded in the principles of an ideological model of literacy education (Street, 1984), and one that affirms the principles of children's rights. Regrettably, these were hardly witnessed during the three weeks of observation in the three schools. As Street (1993) contends, a new literacy studies perspective places pressure on 'what counts as literacy at any time and place asking 'whose literacies' are dominant and whose are marginalized or resistant' (p. 77). The three Maltese state schools prioritised the use of commercial textbooks, workbooks and worksheets, copying without authentic purpose and imparted a universal set of writing skills underpinned by a narrow definition of early literacy learning. From a postcolonial lens, the boys' reactions and opinions show that a highly formalised approach to writing at the age of five is marginalising the 21st- century social and cultural literate worlds these boys experienced outside school. Thus, as with reading, the dominant view of the more powerful – the adults – prevails in early writing practice within the three Year 1 classrooms concerned.

Through a child's rights lens, it can be argued that a writing approach that does not view children as co-participants in learning is impeding access to quality early literacy pedagogy (Articles 12, 13 and 28, United Nations, 1989). The focus on such dominant and decontextualised literacy tasks in early writing curricula is also limiting educators' possibilities to reconceptualise early literacy pedagogic practice in their classrooms and act in the best interests of the children entrusted in their care (Article 3, United

Nations, 1989). The boys' views on early writing contribute to the existing knowledge on boys' underachievement in literacy attainment as it exposes how dominant early writing pedagogical approaches are limiting young boys from experiencing writing in meaningful contexts and through their right to play (Articles 31 and 13, United Nations, 1989) – the way young children learn best (Gray, 2013; Nutbrown, 2014; Roskos & Christie, 2007). The re-examination of boys' voices from this case study echoes an urgent call for rethinking and recopentualising writing in the early years scenario. The need for writing instruction to be decolonised within a postcolonial ECEC practice in Maltese schools and similar contexts is long overdue.

Challenging the colonisation of young minds

Re-examining the young boys' views on reading and writing through a children's rights and postcolonial theory triggered further questions: How is literacy pedagogy in Maltese early primary classrooms playing a role in colonising young minds? How can this be challenged? A top-down education system that focuses on testing in upper primary grades and secondary schools in the Maltese education system lessens the possibility for educators to assist young children in developing critical thinking skills, problem-solving skills and fully engage in dialogue. In the work of Roskos and Christie (2007), we see how the combination of play and literacy allows for the nurturing of such invisible competences that are so important for the success of all children in education and life. With Wolstein (2017), I developed an interest in 'exploring how we can decolonize assessment in order to decolonize curriculum, and then, the mind' (p. 1). This is where Friere's (1970) banking education (see Figure 3.1) concept fits in the re-examination of the boys' views through the dual lens of children's rights and postcolonial theory.

The boys' overall experience of schooled reading and writing is embedded in an educational environment conducive to the depositing of letter-sound relationships in their brains and the repetitive copying of words. The evidenced form of 'banking' (Freire, 1970) early literacy education made visible how this authoritarian process made the boys feel passive, powerless and conditioned to accept the status quo of what counts as literacy for the adults, culture and the postcolonial context they live in. Thus, contemporary 21st-century schooled reading and writing practices experienced by the boys in the three Maltese state schools are not effectively meeting the early literacy learning needs of all postcolonial young male learners. Freire (1970) perceived education as the key to critical spirit and creativity, and banking education as preventing learners from knowing the world around them and consequently promoting passivity. Similarly, the boys in this case study were not allowed to experience reading and writing in ways that embrace their

LA CLASE II

Figure 3.1 The concept of 'banking education'

Source: Memo cartoonist Guillermo Argandoña Sánchez, Mexico, CDMX, from his book *La Clase primera parte*

prior knowledge, freedom and liberty. Freire (1970) challenges the enduring banking education model of education by proposing a problem-posing model of education where both educators and learners co-create and co-construct a learning journey that sustains dialogue, discussion and analysis concerning their emotional state, experiences and knowledge of the world. Friere refers to this process as 'conscientisation' (Freire, 1973). In the context of this study, this implies that: (i) young children do not need answers to problems but opportunities to critically think as they experience meaning and purposeful school-based early literacy learning, and (ii) educators and other stakeholders in education need to challenge their own perceptions of a banking early literacy education model. If we continue holding on to this legacy of depositing information and colonising young minds, through early literacy education, how can we then expect all boys to be critical thinkers and active rather than passive citizens in our society when they turn sixteen or eighteen? Banya's (1993, pp. 166–167) claim supports this argument:

> Much follows, however, from what comes with literacy and schooling. The perspectives, values and assumptions built into school-based literacy practices are often left implicit, thus empowering those mainstream children who already have power and disempowering those children who do not.
>
> (Cazden, 1987; Cook-Gumpers, 1986; Heath, 1983)

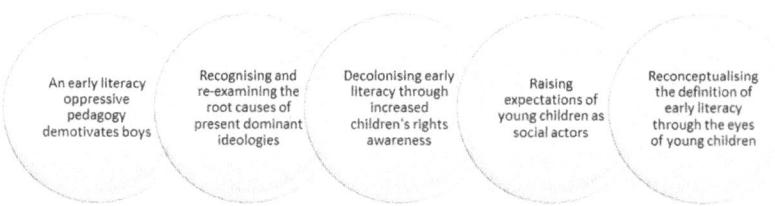

Figure 3.2 The five key takeaways from the boys' views on early literacy in three Maltese state schools

Key takeaways

This chapter concludes with five key takeaways (see Figure 3.2) emanating from the views of five- to six-year-old boys on schooled reading and writing. Each takeaway is unpacked and framed within Freire's (1973) concept of praxis as an invitation to reimagine and hopefully create change through the process of reflection and action.

■ *An early literacy oppressive pedagogy demotivates boys*
  Reflection: This study has shown that schools may be demotivating some young boys from becoming passionate about early reading and writing through the promotion of literacy pedagogies that are underpinned by dominant ideologies that privilege the adult over the child. A re-examination of the findings surfaces the inscribed ties to a colonial past by outlining the overall negative impact that schooled reading and writing had on the young boys in modern Maltese society. The young participants' voices in this chapter are a wake-up call for adult stakeholders in education who blindly accept early literacy learning grounded in a colonial mindset or as I would describe, 'the early literacy oppressive pedagogy'.
  Action: The presented boys' views suggest a transformation from the narrow focus of decontextualised, teacher-led literacy instruction towards a broader conceptualisation of meaningful and decolonised early literacy learning. Stakeholders in education need to take up a diversified view of early literacy in contexts that hold on to a colonial legacy in the instruction of languages. This identified need takes us back to Freire's (1970) concept of 'codification'. Stakeholders can explore and redefine literacy through codifications (visuals) built on gathered information to trigger discussion and engender awareness (Freire, 1988) about oppression in early literacy pedagogy. In the process of 'decodification' individuals identify with the concerned situations and engage in critical reflection to create new understandings for change.

■ *Recognising and re-examining the root causes of present dominant ideologies*
Reflection: Given the boys' evocative voices in this chapter, it is important for pre-service and in-service early childhood educators and other stakeholders in education to develop an understanding of the concept of 'education for conscientisation' (Freire, 1973) and its potential for transformation through the process of critical thinking. According to Friere (1970) it is through 'critical consciousness' that stakeholders in education can recognise, re-examine and reimagine to overcome the persistent legacy of power exerted by dominant ideologies. From a postcolonial lens, stakeholders need to adopt 'an activist position, seeking social transformation' (Viruru, 2005, p. 9).
Action: Stakeholders need opportunites to understand that what is fixed and unjust for young children in literacy education can be transformed into action. This process of critical thinking helps stakeholders in education to imagine new literacy beginnings and realise in practice more equitable, child-centred, rights-based and inclusive early literacy pedagogies; or as Street (1984) refers to, an ideological model of literacy for all children. By implication, they need to start with reflection to view the ideals and cultures of the colonisers and the colonised not as counterparts (Bhabha, 2004), but how these inextricable relationships may be translated, reshaped and transformed in early literacy education.

■ *Decolonising early literacy through increased children's rights awareness:*
Reflection: Boys may be deprived of their right to play, participate actively through democratic early literacy pedagogy and feel included if the focus of early literacy learning is on decontextualised decoding skills in reading and conventional transcription skills and spelling/copying without authentic purpose in writing. This implies that there is a need for the existing relations of power and knowledge reproduction in early literacy learning to be deconstructed and reconstructed through increased awareness of the philosophy underpinning the UNCRC in the field of literacy education and ECEC. How can we challenge Maltese boys' struggling literacy rates if we continue to promote an inherited traditional and inequitable model of teaching reading and writing in the early years?
Action: The boys' views from a postcolonial early learning environment call for the decolonisation of literacy curriculum and pedagogy in Maltese early primary classrooms. Therefore, they raise the case for a transition to playful, rights-based, community-specific and culturally relevant early literacy learning. The advocacy potential of children's rights may be used to assist in this collective endeavour of reflection and

action within diverse contexts and cultures. As Te One and Dalli (2010) point out, an informed discussion on the topic of children's rights is essential to develop a critical ecology amid the early years workforce.

■ *Raising expectations of young children as social actors*
Reflection: Children's views are to be considered respectfully (Article 12, United Nations). The boys' voices suggest that stakeholders in ECEC contexts need to provide an empowering school environment where they are given agency in literacy learning. Thus, stakeholders need to raise their expectations of young children (Bonello, 2020) as social actors and embrace child participation (Articles 12 and 13, United Nations, 1989) in research, policy and practice. As this chapter shows, child participation in research may serve as a valuable source of information to longstanding debates and contentious topics such as boys' underachievement in literacy attainment and the teaching of reading and writing in the early years.
Action: More participatory research with young children is necessary to create new understandings of both boys and girls' early literacy learning experiences within diverse contexts. There is the need for a reconceptualisation of children as powerful agents across societies (Stephenson, 2009). Meeting this demand may pave the way to activate rethinking, refocusing and hopefully overcome enduring barriers to socially just, child-centred, inclusive and collaborative early literacy learning.

■ *Reconceptualising the definition of early literacy through the eyes of young children*
Reflection: The view of literacy as a set of transferable reading and writing skills in current ECEC contexts, overshadowing the importance of listening to and embracing children's sources of knowledge and identity in literacy learning, might demotivate some boys from embarking on their literacy journeys. Countries like Malta, which are bound to a reductionist view of education (boiling down to the perception of early literacy learning as measurement), need to keep their eyes open and listen to what the youngest citizens within the diverse cultures and contexts have to say.
Action: The definition of early literacy education needs to be informed by the perspectives of young children to allow for socially just literacy learning. There needs to be increased awareness of dominant discourses, traditional pedagogies and early testing that impede such democratic school-based early literacy practice through the eyes of young children. Teacher education, both pre-service and in-service, needs to explore ways of teaching and learning that embrace all children's sources of knowledge and child participation (Article 12, United Nations, 1989).

Ultimately, all stakeholders need to listen to what the communicative power of young voices is indicating, and orchestrate collective action in higher-education institutions, organisations, schools, homes and the wider public arena.

In this chapter, the boys' views call for a process of decolonisation of the mind that translates into honouring children's rights in 21st-century schooled reading and writing practices. If we truly want to act in the best interest of all children (Article 3, United Nations, 1989), narrow and eradicate the gender gap (favouring girls) in literacy achievement and realise children's rights in early literacy learning, we cannot let the voices of these boys fall on deaf ears. This is a matter that concerns them (Article 12, United Nations, 1989) and perhaps other children in other schools. It is time to beat the boredom in early literacy learning.

References

Alloway, N. (2007). Swimming against the tide: Boys, literacies, and schooling – an Australian story. *Canadian Journal of Education, 30*, 582–605.

Banya, K. (1993). Illiteracy, colonial legacy and education: The case of modern Sierra Leone. *Comparative Education, 29*(2), 159–170.

Beam, S., & William, C. (2015). Technology-mediated writing instruction in the early literacy program: Perils, procedures and possibilities. *Computers in the Schools, 32*, 260–277.

Bhabha, H. K. (2004). *The location of culture*. London; New York: Routledge.

Boardman, K. (2019). The incongruities of 'teaching phonics' with two-year-olds. *Education 3–13, 47*(7), 842–853. https://doi.org/10.1080/03004279.2019.1622499.

Bonello, C. (2010). *Kinder text zones in the 21st century: Popular culture, media and technology in Maltese homes* (Master's thesis). University of Sheffield.

Bonello, C. (2018). *Boys and early literacy learning in three Maltese state schools* (PhD thesis). University of Sheffield.

Bonello, C. (2019). A paradigm paralysis? Boys and early literacy learning in three Maltese state schools. *Malta Review of Educational Research, 13*(1), 79–107.

Bonello, C. (2020). *Raising expectations for children.* Times of Malta. https://timesofmalta.com/articles/view/raising-expectations-for-children-charmainebonello.815775

Bonello, C. (2021). Democracy or legacy? Boys' views on early literacy in three Maltese state schools. *Journal of Early Childhood Research*, 1–15. https://doi.org/10.1177/1476718X211051330

Bowers, J. S. (2020). Reconsidering the evidence that systematic phonics is more effective than alternative methods of reading instruction. *Educational Psychology Review, 32*, 681–705. https://doi.org/10.1007/s10648-019-09515-y.

Browne, A. (2008). Developing writing in the early years. In J. Marsh & E. Hallet (Eds.), *Desirable literacies: Approaches to language and literacy in the early years* (pp. 81–102). SAGE.

Cambria, J., & Guthrie, J. T. (2010). Motivating and engaging students in reading. *The Nera Journal, 46*(1), 16–29.

Campbell, S. J., Torr, J., & Cologon, K. (2014). Pre-packaging preschool literacy: What drives early childhood teachers to use commercially produced phonics programmes prior to school settings. *Contemporary Issues in Early Childhood, 15*(1), 40–53.

Carrington, V. (2005). New textual landscapes, information and early literacy. In J. Marsh (Ed.), *Popular culture, new media and digital literacy in early childhood* (pp. 13–27). Routledge.

Castles, A., Rastle, K., & Nation, K. (2018). Ending the reading wars: Reading acquisition from novice to expert. *Psychological Science in the Public Interest, 19*, 5–51. https://doi.org/10.1177/1529100618772271.

Cazden, C. (1987). *Classroom discourse: The language of teaching and learning.* Portsmouth, N.H: Heinemann.

Cigman, J. (2014). *Supporting boys' writing in the early years.* Routledge.

Clark, C. (2016). *Children's and young people's writing in 2015.* National Literacy Trust.

Clark, C., & Teravainen, A. (2017). *Writing for enjoyment and its link to wider writing.* National Literacy Trust.

Cook-Gumperz, J. (1986). *The Social Construction of Literacy.* Cambridge: Cambridge University Press.

Cook-Sather, A. (2002). Authorizing students' perspectives: Toward trust, dialogue, and change in education. *Educational Researcher, 31*(4), 3–14. https://doi.org/10.3102/0013189X031004003

Curry, D. L., & Cannella, G. S. (2013). Foreword – Re-conceptualist her/histories in early childhood studies: Challenges, power, relations and critical activism. In V. Pacini-Ketchabaw & L. Prochner (Eds.), *Re-situating Canadian early childhood education.* Peter Lang.

Directorate for Quality and Standards in Education [DQSE]. (2009). *National policy and strategy for the attainment of core competences in primary education.* Ministry for Education, Culture, Youth and Sport. https://education.gov.mt/en/resources/Documents/Policy%20Documents/Attai%20Core_Competencies.pdf

Dyson, A. H. (1997). *Writing superheroes: Contemporary childhood, popular culture, and classroom literacy.* Teachers College Press.

Einarsdottir, J. (2005). We can decide what to play! children's perceptions of quality in an Icelandic playschool. *Early Education and Development, 16*(4), 469–488.

Fletcher, R. (2006). *Boy writers: Reclaiming their voices.* Stenhouse.

Freire, P. (1970). *Pedagogy of the oppressed.* New York: Seabury Press.

Freire, P. (1973). *Education for critical consciousness.* Seabury.

Freire, P. (1988). The adult literacy process as cultural action for freedom and education and conscientizacao. In E. R. Kingten, B. M. Kroll, & M. Rose (Eds.), *Perspectives on literacy* (pp. 398–409). Carbondale.

Gray, P. (2013). *Free to learn: Why unleashing the instinct to play will make our children happier, more self-reliant, and better students for life.* Basic Books.

Griffiths, M. (2012). Why joy in education is an issue for socially just policies. *Journal of Education Policy, 26*, 655–670.

Hammett, R. F., & Sanford, K. (2008). *Boys, girls and the myths of literacies and learning.* Canadian Scholars.

Heath, B. (1983). *Ways with words: language, life, and work in communities and classrooms.* Cambridge: Cambridge University Press.

Hernandez-Zamora, G. (2010). *Decolonizing literacy: Mexican lives in the era of global capitalism.* Multilingual Matters. 10.21832/9781847692641.

International Reading Association (IRA). (2000). *Making a difference means making it different: Honoring children's rights to excellent reading instruction.* Author. https://files.eric.ed.gov/fulltext/ED442081.pdf

Lansdown, G. (2004). Participation and young children. *Early Childhood Matters, 103,* 4–14.

Levy, R. (2011). *Young children reading at home and at school.* SAGE.

Marsh, J. (2005). *Popular culture, new media and digital literacy in early childhood.* Routledge Falmer.

Martino, W. (2008). Male teachers as role models: Addressing issues of masculinity, pedagogy and the re-masculinization of schooling. *Curriculum Inquiry, 38*(2), 189–221.

Mermelstein, L. (2006). *Reading/writing connections in the K-2 classroom: Find the clarity and then blur the lines.* Pearson.

Millard, E., & Marsh, J. (2001). Sending Minnie the minx home: Comics and reading choices. *Cambridge Journal of Education, 31*(1), 25–38.

Ministry for Education and Employment [MEDE]. (2012). *A national curriculum framework for all [NCF].* Salesian Press. https://curriculum.gov.mt/en/Resources/The-NCF/Documents/NCF.pdf

Ministry for Education and Employment [MEDE]. (2014). *A national literacy strategy for all in Malta and Gozo 2014–2019.* http://education.gov.mt/en/Documents/Literacy/ENGLISH.pdf

National Reading Panel. (2000). *Teaching children to read: An evidence-based assessment of the scientific research literature on reading and its implications for reading instruction.* National Institute of Child Health and Human Development.

Neu, T. V., & Weinfield, R. (2007). *Helping boys succeed in school.* Prufrock Press.

Newkirk, T. (2002). *Misreading masculinity: Boys, literacy and popular culture.* Heinemann.

Nutbrown, C. (2014, October 20). *The importance of play.* www.nurseryworld.co.uk/nursery-world/opinion/1147532/importance-play.

Pearson, P. D. (2004). *Reading in the twentieth century.* Centre for the Improvement of Early Reading Achievement.

Pratt, N. (2016). Neoliberalism and the (internal) marketisation of primary school assessment in England. *British Educational Research Journal, 42*(5), 890–905.

Pressley, M. (2006). *Reading instruction that works: The case for balanced teaching.* Guildford Press.

Robert-Holmes, G., & Bradbury, A. (2016). Datafication in the early years. In The National Union of Teachers (Ed.), *The mismeasurement of learning: How tests are damaging children and primary education* (pp. 16–17). College Hill Press.

Rogers, M., Dovigo, F., & Doan, L. (2020). Educator identity in a neoliberal context: Recognising and supporting early childhood education and care education. *European Early Childhood Education Research Journal, 28*(6), 806–822.

Rose, J. (2006). *Independent review of the teaching of early reading.* DfES Publications.

Roskos, K. A., & Christie, J. F. (2007). *Play and literacy in early childhood: Research from multiple perspectives.* Routledge.

Rowan, L., Knobel, M., Bigum, C., & Lankshear, C. (2002). *Boys, literacies and schooling: The dangerous territories of gender-based literacy reform.* Open University Press.

Rowe, K. (2005) *Teaching reading: National inquiry into the teaching of literacy.* https://research.acer.edu.au/tll_misc/5/.

Sims, M. (2017). Neoliberalism and early childhood. *Cogent Education, 4,* 1–10. https://doi.org/10.1080/2331186.2017.1365411

Smith, J., & Wilhelm, J. (2002). *Reading don't fix no chevys: Literacy in the lives of young men.* Heinemann.

Stephenson, A. (2009). Horses in the sandpit: Photography, prolonged involvement and "stepping back" as strategies for listening to children's voices. *Early Child Development and Care, 179*(2), 131–141. https://doi.org/10.1080/03004430802667047

Street, B. V. (1984). *Literacy in theory and practice.* Cambridge University Press.

Street, B. V. (1993). *Cross-cultural approaches to literacy.* Cambridge University Press.

Te One, S., & Dalli, C. (2010). The status of children's rights in early childhood education policy 2009. *New Zealand Annual Review of Education, 20,* 13–35.

Tompkins, G. E. (2013). *Language arts: Patterns of practice* (8th ed.). Pearson Education.

United Nations. (1989). *Convention on the rights of the child.* https://www2.ohchr.org/english/bodies/crc/docs/AdvanceVersions/GeneralComment7Rev1.pdf

Viruru, R. (2005). The impact of postcolonial theory on early childhood education. *Journal of Education, 35,* 7–30.

Walsh, G., Sproule, L., McGuinness, C., & Trew, K. (2011). Playful structure: A novel image of early years pedagogy for primary school classrooms. *Early Years, 31*(2), 107–119.

Whitehead, M. (2010). *Language and literacy in the early years 0–7* (4th ed.). SAGE.

Wolstein, A. (2017). *Decolonizing literacy instruction.* https://din.today/news/decolonizing-literacy-education/.

4 'They start to lose the race before they start it'

Re-envisioning education for the under-sevens in Malta

Chapter Overview

The purpose of this chapter is to create new understandings on the impact of a formal approach to schooled early literacy on five- to six-year-old boys in a former British colony context. The chapter re-examines the quantitative findings emerging from the classroom observations, and the qualitative data collected through interviews, questionnaires and focus groups with several stakeholders during my doctoral research study through a children's rights and postcolonial lens. Findings suggest that the majority of the boys experienced low levels of involvement in learning during a highly formalised approach to schooled reading and writing practices in Maltese and English lessons. This outcome questions the quality of early literacy learning and transitions in a postcolonial ECEC context and the right to play and learn in meaningful ways. Additionally, several stakeholders' claims, including parents of boys, early primary teachers, heads of schools and heads of department (literacy), surfaced a similar negative trend: 'a lost race' of how some young boys' experienced literacy at the age of five. This chapter raises the case for a need to roll back the highly formalised approach to literacy practised in many early years educational settings for the under-sevens in postcolonial Malta, and move towards honouring children's rights through socially just early literacy pedagogies. It is hoped that the five key takeaways at the end of this chapter serve as a trigger to stakeholders in a Maltese ECEC education system and beyond – at the political, institutional and individual levels – to choose and act with decolonial thought and honour children's rights in a collective attempt to narrow existing longstanding gaps in educational attainment.

DOI: 10.4324/9781003125525-4

I started my role as an early primary school teacher in Maltese schools (i.e., teaching five- to seven-year-olds) after some twelve years of teaching in kindergarten (i.e., three- to five-year-olds). I have experienced – together with five-year-olds (some were four years nine months in September) – the sudden shift from a play-based to a highly formalised subject-based approach to schooling. It was a school culture shock to me. In most Maltese schools, a typical start to primary school at the age of five (or almost five) is more about staying quiet, a school day boxed in subject lessons, a bell ringing between the lessons, a classroom crowded with textbooks, worksheets and copybooks replacing kindergarten play areas, and children completing their homework, most of which is textbook/worksheet related.

In recent years, in my roles as an education officer and then lecturer at university, I witnessed several early primary school teachers (working with five- to seven-year-olds) and students on teaching practice within the three sectors of Maltese schools (independent, state and church) experience frustration. It was often noted that this tension was triggered through their will to promote an emergent curriculum approach, and the pressure to teach through a highly formalised approach to cover the content in prescribed schemes of work linked to textbooks/workbooks as from Year 1 (i.e., five- to six-year-olds). In 2018, following the introduction of a learning outcomes framework approach in Maltese state schools, early childhood educators started to attend professional development sessions to implement the emergent curriculum in kindergarten practice (three- to five-year-olds). The intent to implement this rights-based, child-centred, inquiry-based and play-based curricular approach has been evidenced in the other two educational sectors church and independent. There seems to be the intention of introducing an emergent curriculum with the five- to seven-year-olds within an early formal start to compulsory and compartmentalised schooling in state schools. Yet, so far this seems to be up to the discretion of some individual early primary school teachers who are striving to promote a more progressive philosophy within the oppression of an inherited traditional approach.

As indicated in Chapter 1, starting school age for formal schooling is five or younger in 12% of countries around the world (three of which are in Europe: the United Kingdom, Malta and the Netherlands). This percentage comprises the four nations of the United Kingdom, and a range of its ex-colonies and protectorates (Palmer, 2016), including Malta. Palmer (2016) questions the decisions of countries that implemented and maintained a starting school age of five, and though she never located any official confirmation, she declared that 'it certainly accords with my own experience of educational politics: international competition and point-scoring are powerful drivers' (p. 12). The Maltese early years education system (zero to seven– years) – with a legacy of more than 150 years under British rule – holds on to a top-down approach that promotes formal compulsory schooling at the age of five. This current situation brings about a devaluation of play for children in this age group, and sustains narrow views of the concept of school readiness and literacy. Within contexts where formal education starts at the age of five or younger, the present downward pressure of academics and literacy testing leads to an excessive focus on conventional reading and writing practices. This might appear daunting for educators working within such contexts to take up the challenge and transform existing practices, influenced as they are by dominant gendered discourses, an excessive emphasis on high-stakes assessment, and a formalised system based on prescriptive syllabi starting in the first years of formal schooling (age five).

The connecting thread between an early start to formal learning, boys, early literacy, play, quality ECEC, children's rights and postcolonial theory

Early literacy development is a predictor of future success in education and life (Hare, 2011; McGill-Franzen, 2010). If early literacy is so important to children's success in education and life, the quality of teaching is paramount in the first years of schooling. The quality of ECEC impacts on children's success in school on a long-term basis (Logan & Sumsion, 2010). Discourse and interest around structural, process and outcome quality has risen high on the agenda of many governments, researchers and service providers at a European and global level (European Union, 2014). For example, in Malta, a new national framework for ECEC (zero to seven years) grounded in the five pillars of the European quality framework (European Union, 2014) has been launched for public consultation in June 2021. Yet, the Maltese government has not recognised the need to seriously invest in high-quality ECEC, the professionalisation of the ECEC workforce and a competent ECEC system embedded within a systemic approach. In an attempt to counteract, in 2016 a registered voluntary association, the Early Childhood Development Association of Malta (ECDAM; ecdam.org), was co-founded by Dr Anna Baldacchino and myself, to strengthen the values, knowledge and skills of early childhood educators and advocate for high-quality ECEC in Malta.

The school starting age controversy impacts on the educational experience for under-sevens in ECEC. Some countries view an inherent traditional and formal approach to learning as a head start to children to raise the standards, particularly to those coming from disadvantaged backgrounds. Yet, concerns about the appropriateness of formal environments and instruction barring access to playful, purposeful and meaningful learning for the under-sevens have been questioned (Palmer, 2016). Such claims are backed by evidence such as Finland, top scorer in statistical findings related to education systems, where learners start school at seven and are given ample opportunity to learn through play. The education systems in Malta, the United Kingdom and the Netherlands start at five, while other education systems in Europe and most countries worldwide start at the age of six. In some countries, like Sweden, children can start early upon their parents' request, and in Germany children can start if they are 'ready' for formal schooling (Times of Malta, 2008). A study carried out by the International Association for the Evaluation for Educational Achievement (IEA) measures reading levels across 30 countries. The outcome revealed that the top ten education systems were economically advantaged and started school at a later age. Findings from two studies in the United Kingdom, the Cambridge-based Primary Review and the National Foundation for Education Research (Nfer), report that an early-starting school age may give children an initial academic advantage but it does not have a positive impact on children's performance at school or later achievement (Times of Malta, 2008).

The foundations of schooling influences children's future academic and social competence (Dockett et al., 2010). Transition to schooling is a global, highly contested topic (Fisher, 2011). It is common for children in Western cultures to experience obscure pathways as they transition from early years settings to formal schooling (Laverick, 2008). The concepts of school readiness and early literacy learning are often seen together as a key aspect of being ready or not ready for formal schooling. The Maltese education system has a school readiness agenda that prioritises the need to measure early literacy perfromance in schools through phonics screening checklists from the age of five (DQSE, 2009). Given the longstanding debates on an early start to formal schooling and literacy testing, transitions, boys' literacy, children's rights in quality ECEC practice and inherited traditional educational approaches, there is the need to gain deeper insights through several theoretical lenses and within particular contexts and cultures. This chapter is an attempt to fill this gap by re-examining parts of the data from the classroom observations, interviews and focus groups, carried out with several stakeholders during my doctoral study through the dual lens of children's rights and postcolonial theory.

An anticolonial examination of the quality of reading and writing practices through five- to six-year-old boys' level of involvement in learning

As explained in Chapters 1 and 2, one week of observations were conducted in each of the three Maltese state schools (see Chapter 1). I recorded my observations by using a self-created observational framework. One section of the observational framework was titled 'Observing boys' level of involvement in this activity'. This section draws on the quantitative data collected through this specific section in the observational framework. Interlinking my personal interests in quality ECEC and literacy pedagogy for the under-sevens in Maltese schools, I opted to use the five-level descriptors (see Figure 1.5 in Chapter 1) of the Leuven scale of involvement in learning (Laevers, 1994) to assess the quality of learning through five- to six-year-old boys' schooled reading and writing experiences. The level of involvement in learning was rated between levels one to five, one being the lowest.

For the purposes of this book, the following discussion attempts to re-examine the quantitative data collected through Leuven scale of involvement in learning. It specifically focuses on uncovering what the boys' level of involvement in learning within their classroom can tell us about what counts as quality reading and writing in a postcolonial ECEC context that holds on to a legacy of an early formal start to schooling. The statistical data collected from the three Year 1 classrooms in Maltese state schools resulted in three similar outcomes. One figure and one table will be presented in this chapter to serve as a visual representation of the overall observed boys' level of involvement in learning in the day to day schooled reading and writing practices during Maltese and English lessons.

Figure 4.1 represents the boys' level of involvement in learning during 23 reading and writing tasks observed during one week in Awwista School (using the five-level descriptors of the Leuven scale of involvement in learning (see Figure 1.5 in Chapter 1).

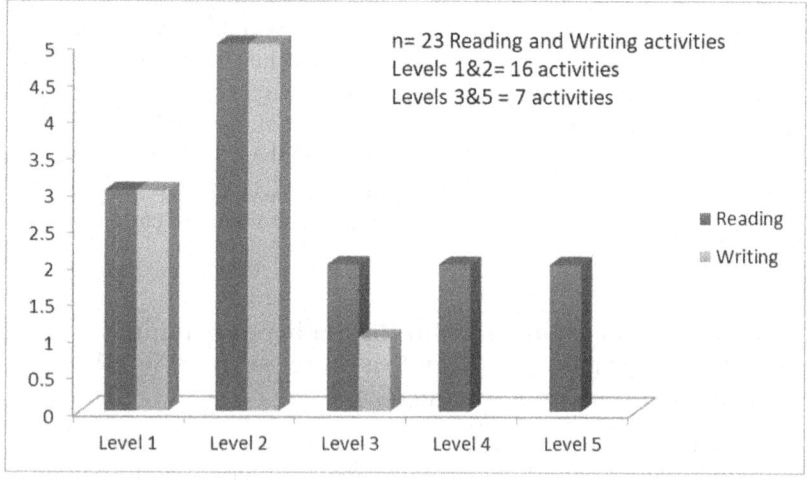

Figure 4.1 The level of involvement in learning of five- to six-year-old boys during reading and writing practices in Awwista School (level one being the lowest)

Table 4.1 explains in further detail the schooled reading and writing tasks five- to six-year-old boys experienced during observation week at Awwista School, as well as their level of involvement in learning. Figure 4.1 and Table 4.1, represent the young boys' low level of involvement in learning during most of the reading and writing practices witnessed during English and Maltese lessons. Even though the Year 1 teachers seemed to prefer a more play-based and child-centred approach to early literacy learning, it was often evident that an academically oriented approach based on the principles of behaviourist theory (Skinner, 1974; Watson, 2013) and a one-size-fits-all (Spiegel, 1998) approach underpinned the literacy pedagogy in this Year 1 classroom. As evident in other research involving boys and literacy, the boys observed in this study were often silenced in an attempt to gain everyone's attention and to complete the assigned reading or writing tasks (Fletcher, 2006; Sax, 2005). On the other hand, as Table 4.1 shows, there were a few instances when the boys were more engaged. For

Table 4.1 Most common reading and writing practices five- to six-year-old boys were involved in during a period of one week in Awwista School

Awwista School *Reading tasks in Year 1 (five- to six-year-olds) and boys' level of involvement (according to the five-level descriptors of the Leuven scale of involvement in learning)*	*Awwista School* *Writing tasks in Year 1 (five- to six-year-olds) and boys' level of involvement (according to the five-level descriptors of the Leuven scale of involvement in learning)*
Spontaneous paired reading between lessons – levels four and five; independent reading between lessons – free choice of books – level four; read aloud session – level three	Writing on copybook (narrow lines) – level two
Phonics and blending consonant-vowel-consonant (CVC) words from interactive whiteboard – levels one and two	Copying sentences from interactive whiteboard – level one
Exposure to print through online rhymes – level three	Writing on workbook – levels two and three
Flashcards and drilling of phonic sounds – level two	Waiting for their turn to write one letter in sand/salt-paint tray – level two
Dialogic reading – level five	Waiting for their turn to write on interactive whiteboard – level two
Core textbook accompanied with songs – level one	Writing the same letter for 36 times on copybook – level one
Maltese grammar and vocabulary taught through PowerPoint presentations displayed on interactive whiteboard – level one	Dictation – spelling test of words studied at home and written at school. Corrected by teacher – level one

example, this happened when the words they were decoding were contextualised and made sense to their experience at that point in time. Reading was being taught in a way that made sense to them and this was also evident through the boys' comments during focus groups (see Chapter 3).

In this study, most boys observed within the three schools struggled to cope with the required tasks and showed passivity particularly when they experienced decontextualised phonics instruction in both Maltese and English, drilling, grammar lessons and copying tasks. Strong teacher control and the expectation of having boys simply being compliant to sit down and carry out teacher-set tasks seemed to be at the expense of nurturing young boys' intrinsic need to volitionally engage in most of the reading and writing practices observed. The attempt to try to work out exercises from textbooks, which seemed to be above their level of competence, made them enter into a world of passivity, making some of the boys yawn. It was annoying for them to stay quiet, as they wanted to talk and express their thoughts. The early writing practices observed were mostly based on conventional transcription skills and spelling/copying without authentic purpose. The 'rubbing off' technique to ensure correct letter formation and spelling was also frequently noted, making most of the boys observed feel anxious and confused. It can be argued that literacy in this classroom was focused more on how reading and writing could be taught and learned in a formal way (Blackledge, 1999) rather than valuing literacy as a social practice (Barton et al., 2000).

The lack of high levels of involvement in learning evidenced during reading and writing practices, questions the quality of literacy education these five- to six-year-old boys were experiencing. Article 29 in the UNCRC speaks to the goal of empowering children to develop their skills. In addition, involvement, together with decision-making, may be perceived as two key features of children's participation (Article 12, United Nations, 1989) in democratic processes (Turnšek, 2009, p. 21 as cited in Lekkai, 2016). The evidence presented above reveals that the boys were being disempowered rather than empowered to develop their early reading and writing skills. Similarly, previous research indicates that traditional approaches are a burden to the brains of boys who turn five as they are not ready to cope with an overflow of formal activities to sit down and learn literacy skills in an explicit way through explicit programmes (Dale, 2008; Shaughnessy & Sanger, 2005). It is important to point out that some of the boys observed seemed to be quicker than others at finishing off their workbooks and copybook tasks. However, they also seemed to display a sense of reluctance and tiredness in such activities.

With reference to the first two years of primary schooling (five to seven years), the Maltese National Curriculum Framework states that the three- to seven-year period must be viewed as the 'formative' rather than a 'formal' period (MEDE, 2012, p. 57). In 2017, data from this study reconfirmed that five- to six-year-old boys in this study were not experiencing the formative period preceding the more formal one in three Maltese state schools. It is also evident that in a Maltese ECEC context, the start of formal schooling at the age of five begets formal instruction of literacy in early primary grounded in centrally imposed English and Maltese syllabi and commended resources (e.g., textbooks) by the state. This is not in line with the aim of the recently implemented learning outcomes framework (DQSE, 2015) approach to pedagogy and assessment practices in the Maltese education system, promising agency and autonomy to schools and educators through a move away from centrally imposed syllabi. In the three Maltese state schools concerned, the observed pedagogy underpinning the reading and writing practices experienced by the boys was mostly bound to commercial programmes to teach systematic synthetic phonics, 'abundant' workbooks, lined copybooks, rubbers, rulers and pencils.

Through a postcolonial perspective, I argue that this is a disguised form of colonialism; a neoliberal approach to the teaching of reading and writing grounded in a market philosophy (Pratt, 2016). This approach is controlling and directing educators' early literacy pedagogies in early primary to cover the content in synthetic phonics programmes and other English and Maltese textbooks. This implies that graduate educators are being forced to teach through textbooks and the test (due to phonics screening tests from the age of five), thus unconsciously supporting a neoliberal market-driven philosophy authorised by the state, as reported in recent research (Boardman, 2021). I argue that this is one example of 'hidden imperialism'. Originating from the West, hidden imperialism prevents educators in postcolonial contexts and beyond from providing more democratic and socially just early literacy pedagogies that fuel and sustain quality within ECEC practice. Malta, and countries experiencing a similar deadlock, need to invest in the provision of decolonised strong foundations of early literacy learning in an attempt to narrowing the gender gap in literacy attainment and moving towards high-quality ECEC.

Every child should receive a high-quality education (UNICEF, 2009). The intent to promote quality ECEC, social justice and democratic pedagogical principles for the under-sevens through the Maltese NCF policy document in postcolonial times is evident. Yet, classroom observations revealed how traditional schooled reading and writing practices, neoliberal official government circulars, compartmentalised syllabi (MEDE, 2018), a prescribed curriculum and phonics screening checklists (DQSE, 2009) in the early primary, have maintained a conceptualisation of 21st-century literacy 'as if it consists of a set of discrete skills that can be taught in isolation' (Larson & Marsh, 2015, p. 4), or as Boardman (2021) puts it 'because reading is only perceived to be SSP' (p. 2). The recorded boys' level of involvement in schooled reading and writing raises the question: Are we truly serving all children with the quality early literacy education we are meant to provide? After 20 years, the findings above reveal that a key challenge that Sultana (1997, pp. 111–112) had pointed out in his review of Malta's postcolonial education development is applicable to date:

> Indeed, a key challenge for the Maltese education system seems to be the extent to which it is able to respond to both values at the same time, that is, to develop a differentiated system (at the secondary, post-secondary and tertiary level) to cater for distinct learning (and labour market) needs without, however, intensifying social stratification. At a macro level, this implies not only educational, but also economic restructuring for a more equitable distribution of educational, financial and social capital. It additionally implies the recognition that every student has an entitlement for a quality education, and that all students are guaranteed access to a specific minimum standard, with teachers and institutions having a degree of autonomy to modify, extend, and teach using pedagogies which are most appropriate to their talents and to the orientation of their students.

The next two sections will unveil how this lack of philosophical integrity, together with puzzling and incoherent political discourse/information, are influencing the views and literacy practices of educators in the first years of compulsory schooling, boys' parents, heads of school and heads of department (literacy) within Maltese state schools.

Boys, literacy and play in early formal schooling: Colonial history repeats itself pedagogically

In the presented Maltese case study, cooperation and communication were limited during the one week of observations. All boys had to sit quietly and do assignments. Millions of euros are being spent on language and literacy education programmes in Malta, yet some young boys are being told to be quiet and sit down during language learning. What message are we giving to these five-year-old boys through such literacy pedagogy? Is it that it is fine not to speak up or that something is wrong with them if they cannot sit down for a long time? The innate drives of young children need to be nurtured and not disregarded. McGill-Franzen (2016) argues that the teaching of reading needs to be playful and inquiry-driven in order for the literacy skills of five-year-olds to improve.

Play is central to socially just and democratic pedagogies in the early years since it encompasses child participation, interactions, relations, listening to children's voices and meaningful learning experiences. Yet, play was very limited and rarely integrated with reading and writing activities in the three classrooms for five- to six-year-olds. A few minutes of playing with bottle caps with letters, letter cards or writing a letter in a salt tray was considered as the playtime of the day. During such moments, an increase in the boys' level of involvement in learning was observed. Throughout the interviews with educators, it was made clear that this was time for 'play', and that they had to hurry up so as to start their 'work' with the workbooks and copying on copybooks:

> My sessions are all with visuals, group work and then end up always with writing in copybooks and workbooks, that's their work; they know it's not time to play.
>
> Ms Miriam, Year 1 teacher, Rużetta School

Literature continues to show that the inclusion of play in classrooms facilitates language and literacy learning (Roskos & Christie, 2007; Whitehead, 2010) and increases children's level of engagement (Laevers, 2000). Yet, in this study, an imbalanced pedagogical approach to reading and writing, mostly teacher-led, where lots of repetition, chanting of letter sounds and drilling took place, prohibited the young boys from their right to learn literacy in the way they learn best – play (Article 31, United Nations, 1989). Indeed, some boys from Awwista School were often asking for outdoor time or to be excused during reading and writing practice.

Having said this, Year 1 teachers' efforts and desire to integrate some components of a balanced literacy approach to the teaching of reading and writing within the existing curriculum-centred system in early primary school was evident. Due to this early start to formal early literacy learning, the boys in this study were also missing out on the effective evidence-based opportunity to develop their competences with new technologies (Labbo & Reinking, 2003; Marsh, 2005; Kress, 2003). Observations revealed that new literacies were being shelved while literacy practice centred around the acquisition of print during the crucial first year of compulsory schooling in the three Maltese state schools concerned. This finding aligns with other national and international research that has also shown how literacy tends to be narrowly defined in 21st-century educational practice (Darmanin & Levy, 2021; Luke & Luke, 2001; Marsh, 2007). This does not imply that educators in this study devalued the importance of play in children's learning:

> On a Friday I like to clean the tables and give them the blocks; they build communicate and share. I think this is a crucial factor. There were boys who were so excited and engaged, using the rolling pin, who knows, maybe this year I can use the play dough to form letters.
>
> Ms Rita, Year 1 teacher, Sawrella School

Educators in the three Maltese state schools showed that the required accountability requirements in relation to the prescriptive and centralised English and Maltese syllabi, in addition to the phonics screen checklists, constrained play to short letter structured activities or once a week 'free play' time. Likewise, the struggle to fit play within timetabled reading and writing work was also evident in other studies (Rogers & Evans, 2008; Waite et al., 2011). Rogers and Lapping (2012) argue that discourses on play pedagogy within policies, practice, teachers' accounts and young children's structured activities tolerate a misconception of instruction and control. In Solsken's (1993) study, similar tensions were also evident between invisible pedagogies (play-centred approach) in the classroom and the home-visible pedagogies (literacy instruction) in relation to early literacy learning. In this study, parents confirmed that their sons preferred to learn through play at this age by explaining the way they strived to transform formal Year 1 homework tasks (mostly related to schooled reading and writing practice) into play activities at home. This, they declared, made it enjoyable for their young boys:

> All the homework tasks that I try to do with him, I try to do them through play so it is enjoyable, even though it is challenging.
>
> Ms Lara, parent, Awwista School

However, not all parents valued play as the medium to learning in the early years, they preferred an ECEC system that is a preparation for Year 1. One head of school pointed out the need for more hands-on play in young children's learning and her wish to change existing cultural beliefs and assumptions about the role of play in schools:

> Learning, although we do a lot of activities hands-on, but I have a dream, I don't want that these activities are one-offs, these should be a daily thing . . . but unfortunately, it takes a lot of money, it takes a lot of culture change, you have to change minds.
>
> Ms Lina, Head of School, Awwista School

Malta survived the colonisation period. Yet, the legacies in different shapes, sizes and forms remain. Said (2003, p. 6) highlights the complex struggles of colonialism 'because it is not only about soldiers and cannons but also about ideas, about forms, about images and imaginings'. The evidence presented in this section reveals that an early start to formal learning is colonising play-based pedagogy in schooled reading and writing practices. The right to play in ECEC (Article 31, United Nations, 1989) and imposed formal early literacy instruction/ work tensions that arise from the presented findings, generates potential for change and transformative pedagogical possibilities (Somerville, 2013) in early literacy learning for the under-sevens in Malta and similar contexts.

**Neoliberal principles of accountability and testing
and its influence on successful reading, writing and
transitions for boys experiencing formal schooling at the
age of five**

During individual interviews, one Year 1 teacher pointed out that two of the
boys go to complementary literacy pull-out sessions because they struggle
to cope with the school's literacy requirements influenced by the existing
early primary centralised syllabi and Maltese and English literacy checklists
(DQSE, 2009). Both boys turned five in November, so they were the youngest in class. She also noted that another two boys managed to cope with the
literacy work done in class, but they had turned six in January (eldest in class).
This evidence sheds further light on the school-starting age debate and the
harm on children's learning, particularly boys, when formal schooling starts
early (Gropper et al., 2011; Palmer, 2016; Whitmire, 2010). From a postcolonial lens, it also reveals how a universal approach to early literacy learning leads to the labelling of children as having literacy difficulties through
assessments grounded in the neoliberal principles of universal testing engen-
dering comparison, rather than authentic strengths-based assessment that
view children as unique. In this section, the presented stakeholders' views
provide real-life examples of how such hidden top-down pressures impact on
some young boys' success with reading and writing and transitions.

Boys and reading at five in formal schooling

Several professionals in schools commented on the lack of books that are attrac-
tive to young boys in the early primary classrooms of Maltese state schools:

> I think we need more books for boys. The phonics books we have the
> decodable ones, these are all related to something like 'Mum's this' and
> 'Mum's that', you know what I mean, for boys these are not attractive.
>
> Ms Miriam, Year 1 teacher, Rużetta School

As the young boys' claimed (see Chapter 3), most adult stakeholders in this
study stated that young boys seemed to favour non-fiction books and other
books that match their interests but these were not easily available in their
classrooms. Parents and teachers shared their diverse experiences as well as
concerns for the boys' ability to blend sounds and read, and their motivation
towards reading at this early stage:

> If boys see reading as boring from the age of five, it's not good. There
> is no enthusiasm at all.
>
> Mr Mauro, parent, Rużetta School

Most of the comments revealed that the boys were not ready to blend sounds or read fluently at this stage, and this reading practice concerned most of their parents. Year 1 teachers were also aware that these books were challenging for some boys to read independently. Other parents pointed out the lack of storytelling, and fun to read and write at the age of five. On a different note, Ms Connie explained how all boys and girls in her class were engaged and highly motivated when reading took place outdoors:

> I am thinking of when we do a reading lesson outside in the ground instead of in class. Both boys and girls are more engaged. The change of environment makes them feel better . . . We do story telling with big books, yes, they enjoy it, at least they have time to move a bit.
>
> Ms Connie, Year 1 teacher, Awwista School

This study found that teachers did not find much time to read to five- to six-year-old children during their first year of schooling in Maltese state schools. Two main reasons were priority given to phonics programmes in Year 1 and the notion that time spent on skills-based approaches is more effective for the teaching and learning of reading. Some parents surfaced their concerns in this regard:

> There needs to be more story telling in Year 1, and because of their age I think that they can teach reading and writing in a fun way. So, when they grow, they get to like it! At least when they think of reading and writing they see it as exciting and not boring . . . after all they are just five!
>
> Ms Grace, parent, Rużetta School

The amount of time spent reading increases the vocabulary, fluency and comprehension of a child making it a crucial factor in determining the reading outcomes in future years (McGeown et al., 2012). In the focus groups and interviews, most of the parents made reference to SSP programmes in a bilingual context:

> Yes, yes even my son, for example the 'u' for umbrella it makes the 'oo' sound in Maltese, he is getting confused there too. The phonics for us are very strange.
>
> Ms Mary, parent, Sawrella School

Words and phrases such as 'confused' and 'not interested' were prominent in the data, adding to the notion of a negative circle when speaking about the experiences of the majority of the boys and their reading practices. As the boys' views in Chapter 3 revealed, adult participants' declarations show that teacher-led SSP programmes seemed to overpower reading for pleasure and child-centred, meaning-based approaches. On a different note, one early primary educator from the online questionnaire explained how she attempted to adapt phonics instruction to contextualise it and make it meaningful to try and meet the needs of the diverse young children in her classroom. Other attempts to implement components of a balanced literacy approach (MEDE, 2014) seem to be turning into a lost battle for educators to ultimately promote effective early reading practices:

> Everyone in the school including the school management team is satisfied that they are doing one big book and one shared reading lesson every term, and personally that leaves me speechless!
>
> Ms Joanne, Head of Department, literacy, Rużetta School

Moreover, all teachers and some parents from the three schools agreed that the use of technology motivated and engaged boys during their school and home reading practices. Nonetheless, as stated by one head of department (literacy), digital literacy did not seem to be 'much into practice in the early primary years' classrooms of Maltese state schools. The same need was also evident in recent studies where teachers struggled to integrate digital resources into schooled literacy practices (Abrams &Merchant, 2013; Flewitt et al., 2014). Indeed, Alvermann (2001, p. 680) argues that 'the possibility that as a culture we are making struggling readers out of some adolescents who for any number of reasons have turned their backs on a version of literacy called school literacy is a sobering thought'.

Boys, writing and early formal schooling

When it comes to boys and writing, popular concerns among Year 1 teachers, parents, heads of Schools, and heads of Department (Literacy) summed up as follows (see Table 4.2):

Table 4.2 Popular concerns on early writing among Year 1 teachers, parents of boys, and heads of department (literacy)

Emphasis on neat handwriting
The dichotomy between invented spelling and writing in lined copybooks
The old school teaching of writing
Homework and weekly spelling tests as added stress to families and young boys

The concerns highlighted in Table 4.2 and the boys' views on reading and writing (see Chapter 3) were evident in most of the early primary teacher's claims:

Writing . . . we have a lot! Writing is the workbooks and copybooks in Year 1. For both boys and girls these are annoying. It's too much repetition (it was a book filled with dotted letters; each page had over 30 dotted letters). This confuses children especially in our school since we have children speaking different languages. This I think we cannot eliminate as we're forced to do it (pointing at one of the Maltese grammar workbooks). One of the boys last time told me: 'Miss, how boring this is!' What can I tell him? You are right?

Ms Miriam, Year 1 teacher, Rużetta School

Conversely, a few early primary teachers mentioned boys and the joys and pleasures of writing:

In my class, boys love writing more than girls and they write way more, both during structured writing and free writing journals.

Teacher, respondent to online questionnaire

Research has shown that before young children learn how to write conventionally, they are able to independently produce writing that represents their thoughts and understandings (Browne, 2008; Cigman, 2014; Ferreiro & Teberosky, 1982). However, as evident above, room for young boys to express their thoughts through independent and free writing seemed to be limited in their schooled writing experiences of Maltese state schools. The use of commercial textbooks, workbooks, copybooks and worksheets were prevalent.

During the three focus groups, parents also expressed their concerns about their five-year-old boys' resistance to completing the assigned homework and dictation (weekly spelling tests) schooled writing tasks. One of the Year 1 teachers explained the process when it comes to homework and spelling revision:

Maltese homework, for example, if in class we did a row of writing words, the column next to it, on the same page, they do it at home and it is exactly the same for spelling revision purposes. It is always like that.

Ms Rita, Year 1 teacher, Sawrella School

The data in the Maltese case study revealed an emerging common trend when it comes to parents' concerns regarding homework and dictation used as writing practice in Year 1 classrooms, and the impact these two strategies have on five- to six-year-old boys:

My son, when I mention the studying and writing of the school dictation at home he says: 'Uff erġajna'! ('Oh no, not again'!)

Ms Lara, parent, Awwista School

In line with Vatterott's (2009) suggestions for more focus on the quality of homework and efforts to eliminate homework with young children, findings from my study question the effectiveness of homework in the early primary years and its long-term effect on young boys' attitudes towards writing. Nonetheless, it seems that homework will continue to be part of the early primary school curriculum as recently the government launched a national homework policy for all children in Malta and Gozo where it is clearly stated that for early primary children (Years 1 and 2; five- to seven-year-olds) it is ideal to have a maximum of twenty minutes' homework daily (The Malta Independent, 2018). It is apt to ask: will Malta ever reverse the trend towards the formality in the teaching of writing in early education, and undesirable homework (mostly conventional writing tasks) for young children?

It is hoped that such evidence serves as an eye-opener for education systems and stakeholders to be conscious of the effects of neoliberal principles that engender top-down pressures paralysing the definition of reading and writing in today's early education. Decolonising mindsets to embrace perceptions of how reading and writing are understood in a digital age (Darmanin & Levy, 2021) and increasing the awareness of every child's right to learn how to read and write in meaningful ways is key to move forward in providing authentic reading and writing experiences for young boys and girls at school. All children have the right to develop their full potential when it comes to reading and writing; thus, starting right from the earliest years is crucial (Article 29, United Nations, 1989).

Transitions in ECEC: young boys making an early start in formal and compulsory schooling

Several stakeholders in Maltese state schools viewed the rapid transition to formal schooling at five from contrasting perspectives:

> We have the best teachers in the early years. They do the workbooks themselves of Years 1 and 2. No complaints from parents, business as usual, children are prepared well.
>
> Mr Mario, Head of School, Sawrella School

> In Year 1 they enter the formal routine so these children particularly some boys and those who are at risk of being low achievers, they start to lose the race before they start it because there is the fear of reading and writing and this is being felt in the first year of our primary school system, surely, no doubt.
>
> Ms Joanne, Head of Department, literacy, Rużetta School

From kindergarten to Year 1, they were treated as babies to now you're
an adult! My son tells me he is bored the whole day sitting down!

Ms Grace, parent, Sawrella School

I see the system as very positive, but I think that they make the children
go too fast. For example, dictation every Monday.

Ms Lara, parent, Awwista School

The majority of stakeholders pointed out the sharp transition between
the play-based pedagogy in the kindergarten stage (three to five years)
and the formalised education system (five to seven years) present in
Year 1 in Maltese state schools. Year 1 teachers in all three schools
seemed to agree that not all boys were ready, and so struggled with the
existing formal schooled reading and writing practices. The concern for
readiness or preparation to formalised education in the first years of
Maltese primary schools seemed to make some parents anxious about
whether or not their son was ready, so they react by giving their boys
extra work at home. Yet, it is interesting to note that some stakeholders
overlooked such concerns and viewed this sharp transition to formal
schooling as business as usual. Conversely, this book was written with
the intent to unveil the business-as-usual aspects of gender, early literacy learning, and ECEC. In the same vein, the contributions in the
book edited by Pacini-Ketchabaw and Taylor (2015). 'set out to trouble
the business-as-usual of early childhood education in settler colonial
places' (p. 26).

This study revealed that most of the comments related to school readiness were largely grounded in an empiricist view where young children
were seen as unready for compulsory schooling, and the need to be prepared to succeed and cope with the existing literacy requirements in early
primary. Research shows that there is a strong link between the way school
readiness is perceived, and the future academic and non-academic success
of each child (Arnold, 2004; Reynolds, 2000). It was interesting to note
how some parents' concerns for the well-being and motivation of their sons
emerged alongside their common assumption that their sons were unready
and needed to be prepared to learn. One head of department (literacy) con-
cluded that:

I think that boys are already giving up in Year 1, not to mention earlier
years. There needs to be a better transition from kindergarten to Year 1
so that Year 1 does not remain as formal as it currently is.

Ms Joanne, Head of Department, literacy, Rużetta School

This study revealed that the existing formal education system, and subsequently the rather decontextualised approach to schooled reading and writing practices in the first year of compulsory schooling, is experienced by some five-year-old boys as a shock or emotional turbulence. This unconstructive, academically driven educational and early literacy learning experience – grounded in a banking education model (Freire, 1988) – aligns with recent evidence (Margetts, 2007), and as some scholars agree (Palmer, 2016; Sayers et al., 2012), it affects the well-being of children and the learning and development in long- and short-term academic achievements. Do these findings ring a bell within the longstanding boys and literacy global agenda? If yes, why is Malta still schoolifying ECEC and literacy education for the under-sevens in the 21st century?

In *Decolonizing the mind* Ngugi (1986) highlights that in the postcolonial times the educated remain colonised, and that there is a need to take on the responsibility to decolonise their minds. Similarly, Amin (1990) refers to the concept of 'delinking' from Eurocentric and colonised perspectives. Through this postcolonial perspective, and in view of the presented findings, stakeholders in a Maltese ECEC sector need to take on the task to decolonise their minds and delink from one-size-fits-all, universal approaches to the teaching of reading and writing and other learning experiences for the under-sevens. This banking model (Freire, 1988) of school-based early literacy learning – largely focused on conventional learning, prescribed curriculum and syllabi and a myriad of textbooks – cannot remain the gift to young children who are being perceived as empty vessels without understanding their worlds. Freire (1973) perceived such conventional ways of teaching and learning as a reproduction of the ways in which the elite treated learners – an empty bank account where knowledge should be deposited. Stakeholders' perspectives in this chapter raise awareness of the rat race to learn to read and write through formal instruction in a Maltese ECEC sector, a race that as classroom observations show is slowing down young boys' involvement in literacy learning. All young boys and girls are entitled to experience more authentic and socially just literacy education right from the start (Article 41, United Nations, 1989).

The arguments in this chapter serve as an invitation to countries with a legacy of formal education at the age of five, or an early start to highly formalised schooled literacy, like Malta, to re-envision, rethink, reconfigure and reposition education for the under-sevens. This transformative process might serve as the turning point where the quality of teaching reading and writing to all under-sevens would begin. It is time to act in the best interest of all children within early childhood spaces and places, before it is too late (Article 3, United Nations, 1989).

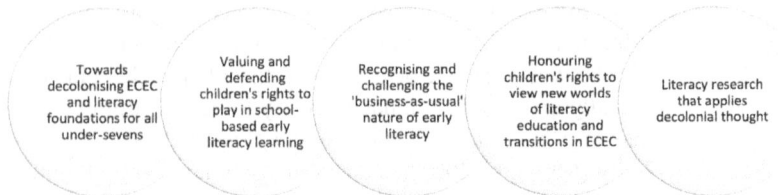

Figure 4.2 The five key takeaways from the boys' level of involvement during reading and writing in three Maltese state schools and several stakeholders' views on young boys, quality ECEC, play and literacy, reading and writing, and transitions

Key takeaways

This chapter concludes with five key takeaways (see Figure 4.2). Each takeaway is unpacked and framed within Freire's (1973) concept of praxis as an invitation to reimagine and hopefully create change through the process of reflection and action:

- *Towards decolonising ECEC and literacy foundations for all under-sevens*
  Reflection: Will Malta take on the challenge of decolonising ECEC and early literacy learning for the under-sevens? This is not a one-man job. Coherent policies and democratic implementation strategies are key to ensure that a highly qualified early years workforce, recognised as professionals, are providing quality early literacy learning within a structure that does *not* place barriers or impose neoliberal agendas in ECEC. Barriers between the early years sector and the community need to be broken to transform ECEC centres into spaces where a shared conception on gender and early literacy may be developed, co-produce knowledge and engage at the same level of interaction and dialogue.
  Action: Educators, families and other stakeholders need to move from a fragmented to a systemic approach in the Maltese ECEC sector. A joint vision needs to be embedded to promote shared responsibility in children's literacy learning and development within state, church and independent school sectors. A systemic approach grounded in coherent ECEC and literacy education policies is essential to meet individual learners' needs and rethink existing universal and compulsory formal early literacy instruction across diverse cultures and contexts.

- *Valuing and defending children's right to play in school-based early literacy learning*

Reflection: Eradicating play in children's lives is violating their rights, and does not help in decreasing mental health problems on a global level. It is time for policymakers and several stakeholders in education to understand the significance of play-based learning in literacy education. It is of the utmost importance to keep advocating and defending the early years (zero to seven years), in Maltese schools and beyond, from rigid, passive schooled literacy practices and formalised curricula.

Action: This chapter calls for policy, research and practice that extols the value of play in literacy learning to keep its significance alive in early years pedagogy for all our youngest citizens to learn and start their school literacy journeys in the best way they possibly could. This is where equity and quality for all young active learners can begin and where lifelong readers and writers flourish.

■ *Recognising and challenging the 'business-as-usual' nature of early literacy*
Reflection: With Wright et al. (2007), this chapter argues that there is a need to trouble 'the taken-for-grantedness of the hegemony of Euro-centric worldviews' (pp. 243–244). The presented findings surfaced the assumed Eurocentrism and a politicised early literacy curriculum, for the five-to-sevens, grounded in a centrally imposed syllabi and commended resources. This form of universalism is depriving some young boys' from being entitled to their human right to quality early literacy education.
Action: Malta needs to reject universal, Eurocentric and colonising epistemologies that penetrate literacy learning and schoolification in ECEC. Spivak (1988) and Wright (2021) view decolonisation as a powerful tool to critique the status quo and not as an alternative. In this light, decolonisation may be integrated with the advocacy potential of children's rights in an attempt to increase awareness and challenge the business-as-usual paralysis in early literacy learning. We need to rethink and reconfigure ECEC and literacy learning for the under-sevens in Malta in the best interest of all children (Article 3, United Nations, 1989). Collective action may assist in the possibility for capacity building through regular multisectoral co-participative approaches as an attempt to understand better children's rights and how to promote more socially just pedagogies (Gale, 2011; Hempel-Jorgensen, 2015; Lingard, 2005; Reay, 2012).

■ *Honouring children's rights to view new worlds of literacy education and transitions in ECEC*
Reflection: Educators in Malta have their own ways of knowing and doing things within their traditional cultures, and they cannot remain in the shadow of universal western knowledge that colonises early literacy curricula and pedagogy (e.g., the SSP programmes adopted in most

schools and the myriad mandated textbooks to teach English and Maltese). Why are we schoolifying ECEC and early literacy learning? Should we not be empowering young boys and girls in early literacy learning, and honouring their rights to quality schooled literacy and smoother transitions whilst developing their full potential? (Articles 3, 29 and 31, United Nations, 1989). For many educators, an espoused theory that is hard to find and realise in practice is social justice (Hackman, 2005).

Action: Children's rights are underpinned by a philosophy that promotes social justice in education. Thus, increasing children's rights awareness in intitial teacher education programmes and ECEC practice may help in moving away from colonised early literacy practice towards more socially-just literacy pedagogies for all. It is the government's responsibility for everyone to know about children's rights and honour them in educational practice, including literacy education in ECEC (Article 43, United Nations, 1989). This may assist in the processes of decolonising literacy pedagogy and curricula for the under-sevens.

■ *Literacy research that applies decolonial thought*
Reflection: The million-dollar question is: Will postcolonial Malta ever realise the NCF's (MEDE, 2012) vision for the ECEC sector – starting formal schooling at seven? This chapter has revealed that the majority of stakeholders and young boys are not in favour of a highly formalised approach to literacy learning at the age of five.
Action: With Wolstein (2017), I agree that more research is needed from academics and educators who feel the need to decolonise literacy practices, particulary for children under the age of seven, and think of new possibile pathways that promote more socially just literacy curricula and pedagogies from the earliest years. Research studies grounded in postfoundational theories (including postcolonial studies), children's rights and reconceptualist work in ECEC, should be considered given the high transformational potential these offer to foster social justice in gender and literacy education.

The evidence presented in this chapter, and the ones before, make a case for a rollback of highly formalised literacy learning in postcolonial education systems for the under-sevens. Out with the old and in with the new, as:

> Children have a right to a good school – a good building, good teachers, right time, good activities. This is the right of all children.
>
> (Malaguzzi, 1993, p. 5)

Not doing so implies that the historical, social, economic, geographical and political elements that shaped the way some boys are experiencing reading and writing at the age of five in 21st-century Malta remains untouched. It is my duty as a passionate academic in the fields of ECEC and literacy, and an active advocate of quality ECEC, to raise awareness about the urgent need to choose and act with decolonial thought, to honour children's rights so as to promote social justice from the roots of literacy education. Changing the pathways of children's literacy learning in future years will be more challenging and costly.

References

Abrams, S., & Merchant, G. (2013). The digital challenge. In K. Hall, B. Cremin, B. Comber, & L. Moll (Eds.), *International handbook of research on children's literacy, learning and culture* (pp. 319–332). Wiley Blackwell.

Alvermann, D. (2001). Reading adolescents' reading identities: Looking back to see ahead. *Journal of Adolescents and Adult Literacy, 44*(8), 676–690.

Amin, S. (1990). *Delinking: Towards a polycentric world*. Sed Books.

Arnold, C. (2004). Positioning ECCD in the 21st century. *Coordinators Consultative Group on Early Childhood Care and Development, 28*, 1–34.

Barton, D., Hamilton, M., & Ivanic, R. (Eds.) (2000). *Situated literacies: Reading and writing in context*. London: Routledge.

Blackledge, A. (1999). Language, literacy and social justice: The experiences of Bangladeshi women in Birmingham UK. *Journal of Multilingual and Multicultural Development, 20*(3), 179–193.

Boardman, K. (2021). Why do early years educators engage with phonics policy directives in their work with under-threes in England? *Policy Futures in Education*. https://doi.org/10.1177/14782103211003221.

Browne, A. (2008). Developing writing in the early years. In J. Marsh & E. Hallet (Eds.), *Desirable literacies: Approaches to language and literacy in the early years* (pp. 81–102). SAGE.

Cigman, J. (2014). *Supporting boys' writing in the early years*. Routledge.

Dale, K. (2008). Early literacy in school: Getting off on the right foot. *Educator's Voice, Journal of Best Practice in Education, 1*, 8–11.

Darmanin, M., & Levy, R. (2021). "It was worth every minute. I'm proud of the way it turned out!" defining reading and writing in a digital age. *Journal of Education and Practice, 12*(26), 1–16. https://doi.org/10.7176/JEP%2F12-26-02.

Directorate for Quality and Standards in Education [DQSE]. (2009). *National policy and strategy for the attainment of core competences in primary education*. Malta: Ministry for Education, Culture, Youth and Sport. Retrieved from https://education.gov.mt/en/resources/Documents/Policy%20Documents/Attai%20 Core_Competencies.pdf

Directorate for Quality and Standards in Education [DQSE]. (2015). *Learning Outcomes Framework* [LOF]. Malta: Ministry for Education, Culture, Youth and Sport.

Dockett, S., Perry, B., & Kearney, E. (2010). *School readiness: What does it mean for Indigenous children, families, schools and communities?* (Issues Paper No. 2). Melbourne, VIC: Closing the Gap Clearinghouse.

European Union (2014). *Proposal for Key Principles of a Quality Framework for Early Childhood Educationand Care: Report of the Working Group on Early*

Childhood Education and Care Under the Auspices of the European Commision.
Brussels: European Commission, DG Education and Culture.

Ferreiro, E., & Teberosky, A. (1982). *Literacy before schooling.* Heinemann.

Fisher, J. (2011). Building on the early years foundation stage: Developing good practice for transition into Key Stage 1. *Early Years: An International Journal of Research and Development, 31*(1), 31–42. doi:10.1080/09575146.2010.512557.

Fletcher, R. (2006). *Boy writers: Reclaiming their voices.* Portland, ME: Stenhouse.

Flewitt, R., Kurcikova, N., & Messer, D. (2014). Touching the virtual, touching the real: iPads and enabling literacy for students experiencing disability. *Australian Journal of Language & Literacy, 37*(2), 107–116.

Freire, P. (1973). *Education for critical consciousness.* Seabury.

Freire, P. (1988). The adult literacy process as cultural action for freedom and education and conscientizacao. In E. R. Kingten, B. M. Kroll, & M. Rose (Eds.), *Perspectives on literacy* (pp. 398–409). Carbondale.

Gale, T. (2011). *Principles from/for social justice policy in Australian education: A potted history.* Paper presented at the Paper Presented at the British Educational Research Association Conference.

Gropper, N., Hinitz, B. F., Sprung, B., & Froschl, M. (2011). Helping young boys be successful learners in today's early childhood classrooms. *Young Children, 66*(1), 34–41.

Hackman, H. W. (2005). Five essential components for social justice education. *Equity & Excellence in Education, 38*(2), 103–109. https://doi.org/10.1080/10665680590935034

Hare, J. (2011). 'They tell a story and there'smeaning behind that story': Indigenous knowledge and young Indigenous children's literacy learning. *Journal of Early Childhood Literacy, 12*(4), 389–414.

Hempel-Jorgensen, A. (2015). Learner agency and social justice: What can creative pedagogy contribute to socially just pedagogies? *Pedagogy, Culture & Society, 23*(4), 531–554.

Kress, G. (2003). *Literacy in the new media age.* Routledge.

Labbo, L. D., & Reinking, D. (2003). Computers and early literacy education. In N. Hall, J. Larson, & J. Marsh (Eds.), *Handbook of early childhood literacy* (pp. 338–354). Thousand Oaks, CA: Sage.

Laevers, F. (1994). *Defining and assessing quality in early childhood education, Studia Paedagogica.* Leuven University Press.

Laevers, F. (2000). Forward to basics! Deep-level learning and the experiential approach. *Early Years, 20,* 20–29.

Larson, J., & Marsh, J. (2015). *Making literacy real: Theories and practices for learning and teaching* (2nd ed.). SAGE.

Laverick, D. (2008). Starting school: Welcoming young children and families into early school experiences. *Early Childhood Education Journal, 35*(4), 321–326.

Lekkai, I. (2016). Children's right to participation in early childhood education. *The Journal of Humanities and Social Sciences, 21*(12), 14–22.

Lingard, B. (2005). Socially just pedagogies in changing times. *International Studies in Sociology of Education, 15,* 165–186.

Logan, H., & Sumsion, J. (2010). Early childhood teachers' understandings of and provision for quality. *Australasian Journal of Early Childhood, 35*(3), 42–50.

Luke, A., & Luke, C. (2001). Adolescence lost/childhood regained: On early intervention and the emergence of the techno subject. *Journal of Early Childhood Literacy, 1*(1), 91–120.

Malaguzzi, L. (1993). *Your image of the child: Where teaching begins.* www. reggioalliance.org/downloads/malaguzzi:ccie:1994.pdf

Margetts, K. (2007). Understanding and supporting children: Shaping transition practices. In A. W. Dunlop & H. Fabian (Eds.), *Informing transitions in the early years: Research, policy & practice* (pp. 107–119). Open University and McGraw Hill.

Marsh, J. (2005). *Popular culture, new media and digital literacy in early childhood.* Routledge Falmer.

Marsh, J. (2007). New literacies and old pedagogies: Recontextualizing rules and practices. *International Journal of Inclusive Education, 11*(3), 267–281.

McGeown, S., Norgate, R., & Warhurst, A. (2012). Exploring intrinsic and extrinsic reading motivation among very good and very poor readers. *Educational Research, 54*(3), 309–322.

McGill-Franzen, A. (2006). *Kindergarten literacy: Matching assessment and instruction in kindergarten.* New York: Scholastic.

McGill-Franzen, A. (2010). The National Early Literacy Panel Report: Summary commentary, and reflections on policies and practices to improve children's early literacy. *Educational Researcher, 39*(4), 275–278.

Ministry for Education and Employment [MEDE]. (2012). *A national curriculum framework for all [NCF].* Salesian Press. https://curriculum.gov.mt/en/Resources/ The-NCF/Documents/NCF.pdf.

Ministry for Education and Employment [MEDE]. (2014). *A national literacy strategy for all in Malta and Gozo 2014–2019.* http://education.gov.mt/en/Documents/ Literacy/ENGLISH.pdf

Ministry for Education and Employment [MEDE]. (2018). *Primary syllabi year 1 to year 6. directorate for learning and assessment programmes (DLAP).* https:// curriculum.gov.mt/en/Curriculum/Year-1-to-6/Pages/default.aspx

Ngugi, W. T. (1986). *Decolonising the mind: The politics of language in African literature.* James Currey.

Pacini-Ketchabaw, V., & Taylor, A. (2015). *Unsettling the colonial places and spaces of early childhood education* (1st ed.). Routledge. https://doi. org/10.4324/9781315771342.

Palmer, S. (2016). *Upstart: The case for raising the school starting age and providing what the under-sevens really need.* Floris Books.

Pratt, N. (2016). Neoliberalism and the (internal) marketisation of primary school assessment in England. *British Educational Research Journal, 42*(5), 890–905.

Reay, D. (2012). What would a socially just education system look like? Saving the minnows from the pike. *Journal of Education Policy, 27*(5), 587–599.

Reynolds, A. J. (2000). *Success in early intervention: The Chicago child-parent centers.* University of Nebraska Press.

Rogers, S., & Evans, J. (2008). *Inside role play in early childhood education: Researching children's perspectives.* Routledge.

Rogers, S., & Lapping, C. (2012). Recontextualising 'play' in early years pedagogy: Competence, performance and excess in policy and practice. *British Journal of Educational Studies, 60*(3), 243–260.

Roskos, K. A., & Christie, J. F. (2007). *Play and literacy in early childhood: Research from multiple perspectives.* Routledge.

Said, E. W. (2003). *Orientalism.* Penguin Classics.

Sax, L. (2005). *Why gender matters: What parents and teachers need to know about the emergence science of sex differences.* New York: Doubleday.

Sayers, M., West, S., Lorains, J., Laidlaw, B., Moore, T., & Robinson, R. (2012). *Starting school: A pivotal life transition for children and their families.* Australian Institute of Family Studies.

Shaughnessy, A., & Sanger, D. (2005). Kindergarten teachers' perceptions of language and literacy development, speech- language pathologists, and language interventions. *Communication Disorders Quarterly, 26*(2), 67–84.

Skinner, B. F. (1974). *About behaviorism.* New York: Vintage Books.

Solsken, J. (1993). *Literacy, gender and work in families and in school.* NJ Ablex.

Somerville, M. (2013). *Water in a dry land: Place-learning through art and story.* Routledge.

Spiegel, D. (1998). Silver bullets, babies, and bath water: Literature response groups in a balanced literacy program. *The Reading Teacher, 52*(2), 114.

Spivak, G. C. (1988). Can the subaltern speak? In C. Nelson & L. Grossberg (Eds.), *Marxism and the interpretation of culture.* University of Illinois Press.

Sultana, G. R. (1997). *Inside/outside schools* (new edition). P.E.G. Ltd.

Times of Malta. (2008). *Early Birds.* https://timesofmalta.com/articles/view/early-birds.196363

The Malta Independent. (2018, March 26). *Government establishes set amount of time children should be spending on homework.* www.independent.com.mt/articles/2018-03-26/local-news/Government-establishes-set-amount-of-time-children-should-be-spending-on-homework-6736186919

United Nations. (1989). *Convention on the rights of the child.* https://www2.ohchr.org/english/bodies/crc/docs/AdvanceVersions/GeneralComment7Rev1.pd

United Nations International Children's Emergency Fund [UNICEF]. (2009). *Child friendly schools manual.* UNICEF Division of Communication.

Vatterott, C. (2009). *Rethinking homework: Best practices that support diverse needs.* Alexandria, VA: ASCD publications.

Waite, S., Evans, J., & Rogers, S. (2011). A time of change: Outdoor learning and pedagogies of transition between foundation stage and year 1. In S. Waite (Ed.), *Children learning outside the classroom: From birth to eleven* (pp. 50–64). SAGE.

Watson, J. B. (2013). *Behaviourism.* London: Kegan Paul, Trench, Trubner & Co., Ltd.

Whitehead, M. (2010). *Language and literacy in the early years 0–7* (4th ed.). SAGE.

Whitmire, R. (2010). *Why boys fail: Saving our sons from an educational system that's leaving them behind.* AMACOM.

Wolstein, A. (2017). *Decolonizing literacy instruction.* https://din.today/news/decolonizing-literacy-education/.

Wright, H. K., Nashon, S., & Anderson, D. (2007). Guest editorial: Rethinking the place of African worldviews and ways of knowing in education. *Diaspora, Indigenous, and Minority Education, 1*(4) 239–245.

Wright, H. K. (2021). Decolonisation and higher education: Theory, politics and global praxis. *Postcolonial Directions in Education, 10*(1), 23–50.

5 Conclusion

This book retells the story about some young boys and literacy in a Maltese postcolonial ECEC context to create a dialogue with other similar educational contexts at a global level. It shares unmasked colonialist tensions that some five- to six-year-old boys and several stakeholders experienced and unconsciously practised in ECEC classrooms within Maltese state schools. Each chapter helps the readers visualise how camouflaged inherited legacies have taken shape in the 21st-century postcolonial education in Malta, colonising some young boys' minds, early literacy learning and the quality of ECEC and literacy curricula for the under-sevens. Some may see this book as negative or deconstructive in nature. Yet, those who lived the need for a reconceptualisation of gender, literacy and ECEC in postcolonial contexts and beyond, view the constructive critique in this book as a sign of hope, of increased possibility and as a starting point from which action can be taken to challenge oppression and marginalisation.

Raising the awareness of the silences brought about through settler-colonial legacies need strong convincing forces that have an impact on postcolonial political agendas. Thus, the advocacy potential of the world's most ratified treaty – the UNCRC (United Nations, 1989) – interweaved with the transformational potential of postcolonial theory, are threaded through the chapters of this book to confront lingering colonial pressures in the fields of gender, literacy and early years education. An attempt to make the unjust known. Each chapter aims to empower stakeholders in education to weather colonialist legacies in policy, discourse and practice as they create and sustain dialogues, debates, reflect and consider new possibilities for collective action:

> Liberation in the Freiran sense is not what a messianic person does for others, but an ongoing struggle of collective conscientization and action mediated by dialogical encounters.
>
> *Reyes and Torres* (2007, p. 90)

DOI: 10.4324/9781003125525-5

In this light, it is worth remembering Antonio Gramsci – 'an iconic figure in 20th century social and political theory' (Mayo, 2015, p. 8). Gramsci's belief that liberation from oppression initiates with education implies that education needs to guide the individual to think critically and independently, to become conscious of their values and responsibilities. Maltese citizens need learning that happens through consciousness raising. These COVID times were a step back to slow down and reflect in the lives of many. Educators, parents, policymakers, researchers and other stakeholders in Malta need to use this time to rethink and play their part to strengthen and sustain strong foundations in education for all children. Moreover, we need to attain an increased critical awareness (Mayo, 2015) of our history, beliefs, rights and obligations concerning children, childhood, literacy education and ECEC and create change. Change cannot happen without hope (Fromm, 1970). Identifying myself as a reconceptualist scholar, I rest this book on the ideology of hope, hopeful that the dual lens of children's rights and postcolonial theory serves as an eye-opener to trigger reflection and action.

In an attempt to answer one question, 'How do different stakeholders' perceptions, including young boys' views and experiences of early literacy learning within a postcolonial Maltese ECEC context, feature through the significant perspectives of children's rights and postcolonial theory?', three key developing arguments and five key takeaways in Chapters 2, 3and 4, offer a space for the concepts of gender, early literacy learning and ECEC to be rethought, reconceptualised and hopefully reshaped, as these settle within decolonised, open, critical and reflexive mindsets. Each chapter concludes with five key takeaways, framed within Freire's (1970) key concept of conscientization. Thus, offering several pathways guided by reflection and action for educators, parents, leaders, academics, policymakers and other stakeholders in ECEC.

Chapter 2 unmasks a need to deconstruct and reconstruct new ways of thinking about boys' underachievement in literacy attainment. It illuminated how constructions of masculinities grounded in a narrow definition of the concepts of gender and literacy, maintain unequal power relationships that may be toxic to boys' negotiations of literate identities. The transpired construct of the male learner as rough, slow and messy in a highly formalised approach to early literacy learning in Maltese state schools fits in the colonial ideology of childhood subservience to adult power. This inherited hidden will to power is essentialising the way the majority of participants' view gender as a binary, and literacy as a cognitive skill to read and write. Accepted myths of gender as biologically unchanging and fixed need to be challenged (MacNaughton, 2000). Thus, this chapter points out the need for critical literacy (Freire, 1985) and ongoing dialogue between all stakeholders in education to redefine what it means to be male and female, uncover existing challenges grounded in historical roots and explore new avenues for gender equity approaches to early literacy education. To conclude, Chapter 2 argues that the advocacy potential of the UNCRC may serve as a tool for postcolonial stakeholders in education to contest political and social oppression in gender and schooled early literacy education. Ultimately, ECEC is to offer all children, as citizens, their right to non-discriminatory literacy practice (Article 2, United Nations, 1989) within postcolonial contexts, and any other time, space and place.

In Chapter 3, the boys' perceptions on reading and writing practices make visible what counts as school-based early literacy learning in three Maltese state schools. It shows how young minds may be colonised through authoritarian and decontextualised early literacy, which largely focused on the rote learning of letter-sound relationships and copying tasks. The boys' views point to a need for the rebalancing of power relations in the teaching of reading and writing. As Te One (2011) writes: 'How to balance this power depends on how children are consulted or listened to about matters that concern them – a point expressed in Article 12 of UNCROC' (p. 1). In this light, Cannella (1997) describes how content knowledge that constructs ECEC tends to silence the voices and ways of being of the young children and families concerned, the 'voices of silent knowing' (p. 10). Sharing the boys' voices in this book is an act to break the silence of young children in literacy education, an act in their best interest (Article 3, United Nations, 1989). The chapter highlights that a reconceptualisation of early literacy learning, particularly the teaching of reading and writing, may be addressed through the advocacy potential of children's rights, and provide opportunities for all stakeholders in ECEC to:

> deconstruct the decolonization complexity and reconstruct a theory of postcolonial citizenship education . . . This means that to be effective, decolonization theories and interventions must address the problematic of postcolonial consciousness – as a social construct and the starting point of reflection.
>
> Barongo-Muweke (2016, pp. 5–6)

Childhood is not a phase in life to speed up. Chapter 4 critiques the operations of power – a colonial reproduction – ingrained in a formal approach to the teaching of reading and writing sustaining Eurocentric literacy knowledge and practice in postcolonial times. We need to protect the developing minds from the risk of building weak literate identities and dispositions towards literacy learning under the age of seven. Young children cannot remain silent in the shadows, positioned as the colonised within early literacy education. Also, educators working with five- to seven-year-olds within a formalised approach to schooling cannot remain still in an ECEC system that promotes centrally imposed syllabi, usurping their agency and autonomy as professionals in the field. There is a pivotal need for other ways of knowing that also embrace native perspectives as an alternative to the Eurocentric literacy pedagogy imposed in Maltese and English language classrooms from the age of five in Malta. Wright (2021) states that 'Decoloniality is about delinking from the hegemonic game and constructing and participating in a new game' (p. 28). The advocacy potential of the UNCRC may serve as the trigger to meet this longstanding need.

With this in mind, the overall evidence in this book and the national attitude to early literacy learning raises the case for a rollback in the formal start to learning at the age of five in a Maltese postcolonial context. Palmer (2016, p. 9) reminds us that 'the western nations that *do* shine in international surveys have a school starting age of seven'. The voices of young boys and several stakeholders in this book are telling us that we need to think the world order of an early formal start to schooling at five differently. Stakeholders in education need to value and recognise play-based learning, also in literacy education, and raise their awareness about Eurocentric, colonialist, and colonising discourse, praxis and early literacy learning deriving from distorted knowledge.

Throughout Chapters 2, 3 and 4 it is argued that more research is needed to fuel current policies and practices in the foundations of postcolonial education systems and across the globe. There is more to be learned about gender and literacy attainment in early childhood within diverse contexts:

- There is a need to understand how girls are experiencing literacy within postcolonial ECEC contexts. Also, new research is needed to create new knowledge that helps us unthink what we think we know, and what we take for granted, about boys and girls and literacy across diverse cultures and contexts. ECEC sectors of diverse contexts need to localise postcolonial mental models in gender and early literacy education.

- This book calls for scholars to focus their developing research in reconceptualist work in ECEC to narrow the gaps of social justice in educational practice. More research that embraces a child's rights lens and postfoundational theories (e.g., postcolonial, poststructural, postmodern etc.) need to be recognised and valued given the advocacy and transformational potential of these movements at a global level.

- Last but not least, this book hopes to inspire and help other education researchers to develop the skills needed to recognise, value and include young children's participation (Article 12, United Nations, 1989) in research that pertains to the fields of gender, literacy and early childhood.

As societies and policies change, stakeholders working in the fields of literacy and ECEC, and also children, need to understand the importance of the UNCRC and the need to respect each other's rights to move from utilitarian education systems towards rights-based, equal and active citizenship education systems in postcolonial ECEC contexts (Target 4.7 of the 2030 Agenda for Sustainable Development, United Nations, 2015). In a Maltese context, while several efforts to realise children's rights in practice are underway (The Malta Foundation for the Wellbeing of Society, 2014; The Children's Rights Observatory Malta, 2021), the disconnections between children's rights, law and educational policies and programmes remain. Malta's commissioner for children has recently claimed that the proposed revision of the Education Act is not adequately grounded in the philosophy of children's rights (Times of Malta, 2021). As the presented case study reveals, a unified vision, starting from the roots of the Maltese education system, is needed. It is time to invest more in ECEC (Bonello, 2020, 2021) to strengthen the foundations and move towards a systemic and competent education system that:

■ Addresses a longstanding need for an advisory governance group formed by stakeholder groups and sectors in ECEC to create overarching and coherent rights-based policies (also those concerning literacy education and ECEC). Multisectoral collaboration and action are needed to develop strategic plans that can be effectively implemented through the required policy infrastructure.

■ Offers all pre-service and in-service early childhood educators the possibility to be part of the professionalised teacher's workforce, engage in joint learning, critical reflection and ongoing dialogue (also in partnership with parents). The system needs professionals and leaders in ECEC to monitor and offer continuous pedagogical support.

■ Honours, values and recognises children's rights, including child participation, in policies, law, frameworks and educational programmes, to rebalance power in the fields of gender, ECEC and literacy.

It is hoped that this book will serve as a resource to generate political priority for early investment in ECEC in a Maltese postcolonial context and elsewhere. Furthermore, the rediscovery of Friere's concept of the 'pedagogy of the oppressed' served as guidance for the oppressed to better understand, lead and develop from within critical activism for social justice and the full realisation of children's rights in educational practice.

Yet, the question remains: Will Malta, and countries like it, ever be free from efforts to imitate the West? With Mayo, I contend that 'Colonialism cannot be viewed as a question of "us and them"' (Maltatoday, 2012).

Colonialism and the Maltese culture and identity cannot be separated, neither in literature, discourse nor in reality. This book sought to seek a compromise within a postcolonial early childhood context, as will be represented and summarised through an analogy in the final section.

From unchartered to chartered waters: Another world is possible

> Water does not resist. Water flows. When you plunge your hand into it, all you feel is caress. Water is not a solid wall, it will not stop you. But water always goes where it wants to go, and nothing in the end can stand against it. Water is patient. Dripping water wears away a stone. Remember that, my child. Remember you are half water. If you can't go through an obstacle, go around it. Water does.
>
> Margaret Atwood – *The Penelopaid*

The time to wrap up this book was close when I received the quote above, an extract from the 2005 novella by Canadian author Margaret Atwood, as a text message from a colleague and friend of mine. She sent it to me because water reminded her of me and my passion for the big ocean blue. Reading it made me realise that what I wanted to say in the concluding words of this book fully resonated with Atwood's words above.

This extract made me see water, as a literal and symbolic natural element, that can be used as an analogy to what this book set out to do. This book makes known the story of some young boys and literacy in Malta. It sought to uncover how different stakeholders in one postcolonial ECEC context tried to navigate through the impact of colonialist legacies in the fields of gender, literacy and ECEC within unchartered waters. The past cannot be erased – *water always goes where it wants to go, nothing, in the end, can stand against it* – yet the evidence-based developing arguments in this book provide a space for reflection to raise the awareness that one can choose to navigate through chartered waters. This book was written with the intent to act as a compass, to help you refocus the lens and visualise multiple ways of seeing and understanding gender, literacy, children's rights and postcolonial theory. You need to develop the courage needed to move away from seeing colonialism as the impasse – *If you can't go through an obstacle, go around it. Water does.*

Thus, this book invites you to collapse the boundaries between colonial and postcolonial times. Some young boys in this book are experiencing oppressed gender discourse, schooled early literacy, and the ECEC system that is stopping them from becoming fully realised human beings in the world. But *water will not stop you. Water is patient.* Our consciousness as educators, leaders, students, policymakers and scholars in postcolonial contexts is formed within the oppressive order in which we are educated and in which we live. In the struggle for liberation, humanity may be regained, and children's rights may be realised in practice, only if we create an education system led by the oppressed for the oppressed (Friere, 1970). Like *dripping water*, these chapters have offered progressive and pluriversal possibilities, from the local to the global, in the hope to *wear away stones* through the praxis of reflection and action, the process of 'conscientization' (Friere, 1970), to liberate from dominant conscience, and decolonise gender, literacy, and early childhood education. Walter Mignolo's (2011) work in critical education, reminds us that the aim of decoloniality is the birth of new world order and the belief that another world is possible.

There is the need for Malta and countries experiencing similar challenges to reject the current world order for hierarchical gender binarism in early literacy, the schoolification of ECEC and a highly formalised literacy approach for the under-sevens. The change needs to come from within – top-down, imposed quick fixes are not the solution.

References

Barongo-Muweke, N. (2016). *Decolonizing education: Towards reconstructing a theory of citizenship education for postcolonial Africa*. Springer.

Bonello, C. (2020, December 7). Children's needs cannot wait. *Times of Malta*. https://timesofmalta.com/articles/view/childrens-needs-cannot-wait.837125.

Bonello, C. (2021, October 2). Early school leavers and the early years in Malta: Will we ever start from the beginning? *Education Update, 12*. https://issuu.com/unionprint/docs/education_update?fbclid=IwAR1nc9kD_czVK3QSmkOVbCT-TACUqD6JzUOswVpbrSvWvbBEio9rUK8LsQsk.

Cannella, G. S. (1997). *Deconstructing early childhood education: Social justice and revolution*. Peter Lang.

Freire, P. (1970). *Pedagogy of the oppressed*. New York: Seabury Press.

Freire, P. (1985). Reading the world and reading the word: An interview with Paolo Freire. *Language Arts, 62*(1), 15–21.

Fromm, E. (1970). *La revolución de la esperanza: Hacia una tecnología humanizada, trans. D. jiménez C.* Fondo de Cultura Económica.

MacNaughton, G. (2000). *Rethinking gender in early childhood education*. Allen & Ulwin.

Maltatoday. (2012). *To know us is to know the English*. www.maltatoday.com.mt/arts/books/23105/to-know-us-is-to-know-the-english-20121203#.YXKjWS2w2Rt.

Mayo, P. (2015). *Hegemony and education under neoliberalism: Insights from Gramsci*. Routledge.

Mignolo, W. D. (2011). Geopolitics of sensing and knowing: On (de)coloniality, border thinking and epistemic disobedience. *Postcolonial Studies, 14*(3), 273–283.

Palmer, S. (2016). *Upstart: The case for raising the school starting age and providing what the under-sevens really need.* Floris Books.

Reyes, L. V., & Torres, M. N. (2007). Decolonizing family literacy in a culture circle: Reinventing the family literacy educator's role. *Journal of Early Childhood Literacy, 7*(1), 73–94. https://doi.org/10.1177/1468798407074837.

The Children's Rights Observatory Malta [CROM]. (2021, June 24). *Observatory set up to champion children's rights.* https://timesofmalta.com/articles/view/observatory-set-up-to-champion-childrens-rights.881812.

The Malta Foundation for the Wellbeing of Society [MFWS]. (2014). www.marielouisecoleiropreca.com/en/impenji/impenji-lokali/the-malta-foundation-for-the-wellbeing-of-society/

Te One, S. (2011). Defining rights: Children's rights in theory and in practice. *He Kupu the Word, 2*(4). www.hekupu.ac.nz/article/defining-rights-childrens-rights-theory-and-practice.

Times of Malta. (2021). *Amendments to education rules 'not sufficiently child-centred' – commissioner.* https://timesofmalta.com/articles/view/amendments-to-education-rules-not-sufficiently-child-centred.898621

United Nations. (1989). *Convention on the rights of the child.* https://www2.ohchr.org/english/bodies/crc/docs/AdvanceVersions/GeneralComment7Rev1.pdf.

United Nations. (2015). *Transforming our world: The 2030 agenda for sustainable development.* UN Publishing.

Wright, H. K. (2021). Decolonisation and higher education: Theory, politics and global praxis. *Postcolonial Directions in Education, 10*(1), 23–50.

Index